RICHARD CLUBLEY lives in Sheffield which is not a good place to stay if you love Scottish islands. Even so, he makes the journey north several times a year and it is always a thrill. He has visited 65 of the islands and never tires of them. They are all different, beautiful and endlessly fascinating.

He has led school parties to Staffa; camped on Mingulay and argued with the Laird on Eigg. He has seen rare birds on Fair Isle, otters on Mull and kayaked to Pladda.

Richard has visited Britain's smallest secondary school on Out Skerries, found archaeological treasure in Orkney and discussed wind turbines in Shetland. He almost perished on Ailsa Craig and was blown off his feet on Tiree. He met a Bronze Age queen on Bute and enjoyed Lady Monica's bed in Rum (a story not included here). He hasn't made it to Shiant – yet – but saw pink dolphins off St Kilda.

LIZ THOMSON trained as a teacher before taking up her brush and pencils and graduated from Sheffield School of Art in 1979. Her work is regularly exhibited both locally – in Sheffield, where she still lives – and nationally. Liz won a major prize for landscape in the 2001 Laing competition and was a regional finalist in the 2005 competition for Channel 5. Her work hangs in private collections in the USA, Holland, Austria and France, as well as here in the UK.

Scotland's Islands

A Special Kind of Freedom

Richard Clubley

RICHARD CLUBLEY

with illustrations by LIZ THOMSON

Luath Press Limited

EDINBURGH

www.luath.co.uk

First Published 2014

ISBN: 978-1-910021-07-1

The paper used in this book is recyclable. It is made from low
chlorine pulps produced in a low energy, low emission manner from
renewable forests.

Printed and bound by
Bell & Bain Ltd., Glasgow

Typeset in 10.5 point Sabon
by 3btype.com

*Dedicated to Nigel Laybourne: schoolteacher,
valued colleague and sea kayaker.
Nigel understands, absolutely, the special nature
of the freedom to be had exploring the
Scottish islands. You can read about one of his
adventures in chapter five.*

Contents

Map 1 – Scotland with all her islands in the right places.

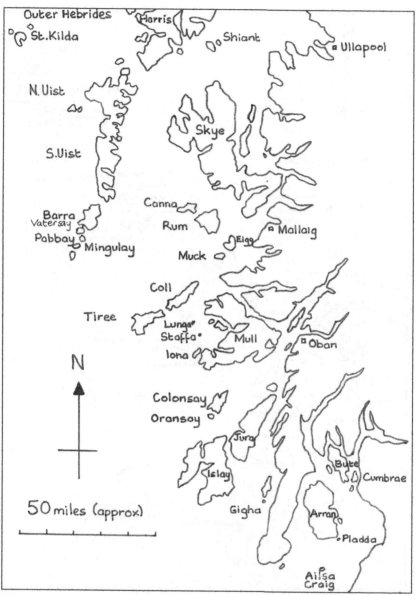

Map 2 – Ailsa Craig to the Outer Hebrides.

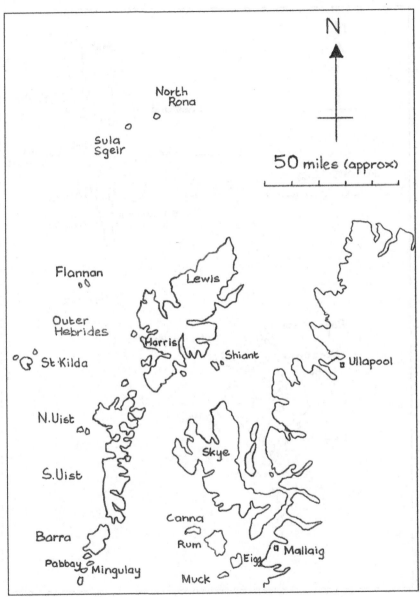

Map 3 – Lewis and the Atlantic outliers.

Map 4 – Orkney and Shetland.

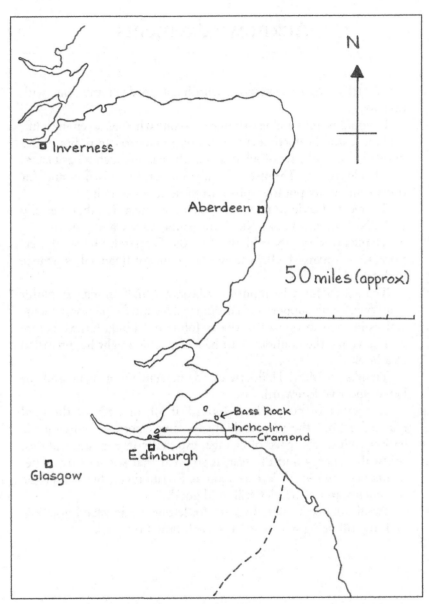

Map 5 – The Firth of Forth.

Acknowledgements

A BIG THANK YOU to everyone who has helped, in any way, with this book.

It would be impossible to name everyone who has given me a lift, told me a story, offered a cup of tea or a place to camp, but please know you are all part of what makes the islands such great places.

Thanks to Liz Thomson for all the tea and biscuits and for transforming my photographs into these super drawings.

Thanks to Gavin MacDougall and everyone at Luath, especially Lydia Nowak and Laura Nicol, for sound advice and guidance.

Thanks to Serco Northlink, Promote Shetland, Orkney Enterprise, Caledonian MacBrayne and Loganair for financial assistance with travel.

Thanks to John Humphries, editor, *Scottish Islands Explorer* magazine, for his support and encouragement and for publishing some stories in the run up to this book. John, and Linda Grieve before him, gave me the confidence to believe people might be interested in a book.

Thanks to Mairi Hedderwick for her encouragement and for her supportive foreword.

A number of people have looked at all, or part, of the final manuscript but the responsibility for any errors or omissions is entirely mine. The pace of change, especially in communications, renewable energy and the rest, is so great that some of my statements may be out of date as soon as I write them, but I hope the sentiments and principles still hold good.

Finally, thanks to Bev, my wife, for letting me go island-hopping, and for still being here – so far – each time I get back.

Foreword by Mairi Hedderwick

LAWRENCE DURRELL IN *Reflections on a Marine Venus* defined the word 'islomania' as a 'rare affliction of the spirit' and 'islomanes' as sufferers from this powerful addiction to islands. *Scotland's Islands* is for all such sufferers; myself being one of the afflicted, long since thralled to the draw of islands.

Richard Clubley has created a random plaid of the Scottish islands. He uses different colours and textures for each island experience. Difference being the essence of an island; that 'sea in-between' defining its individuality. There is honest factual appraisal for some islands woven into emotional and personal responses for others. And everywhere the birds. And islanders, a rare species in their own right.

There is a quirkiness to the author's interweaving reminiscences, some with other islomanes, juxtaposed with analytical studies of current island statistics. It is also a style that gives one island in-depth analysis and a personal and impressionistic brush stroke for another. These are the revealing vagaries of all personal journeys.

This book is full of valuable references for now and for the future. The islands are changing rapidly. Some romantics rue this but our islands are not just made up of sand, sea, wildlife and *machair*. They are also made up of communities carving out livelihoods with limited resources and supply chains – that 'sea in-between'. Given the nature of their diverse island conditions some islands are better placed, geographically and socially, for the necessary development to retain and enlarge their populations. There are some islands that still keep with the past but a compromise can be made and change accepted; that special kind of freedom need not be lost.

Liz Thomson's striking black and white illustrations are strong and direct with an engraving quality to her images which partner the text without sentimentality. So often the art of the illustrator is sacrificed to the colour photograph.

All in all, a book for islomanes to savour in sips. Nightcaps are suggested; that way the addiction can be controlled.

Introduction

MY DICTIONARY DOESN'T LIST 'Islomania' although I think it should. The passion many of us have for islands is well known and documented, so I think there should be a word for it. I don't know when or where or how I caught the island bug but I have it and there is no known cure. All one can do is scratch the itch now and then but that only seems to make it worse. I have been wondering if the condition is innate or nurtured in us.

I was born and raised in Withernsea on the east coast of Yorkshire and I remember my father pointing out Bull Fort, a WWII installation in the mouth of the Humber, when I was about six. It was my first island. I wanted to go and explore it but never did. Forty years later I passed very close to Bull Fort on a ferry out of Hull. It is nothing more than a rust-stained block of concrete but the desire to land and walk around it was as strong as ever.

On summer days in Withernsea we children longed for the tide to go out far enough for Stony Island to be exposed so we could walk out and look for crabs. Stony Island isn't an island at all, it's a featureless heap of pebbles that appears on the beach at low water, spring tides. To us lads it was Atlantis and I still love to see it when I visit.

My first Scottish island was Arran, first visited when I was about eight years old, and I have been in thrall to islands ever since – mystery, inaccessibility, adventure, travel and exploration. In my adult island-hopping I have realised that, no matter how remote, small or inaccessible an island is, there will always be a smaller one, just offshore, and when I get there other people will have been before me.

Islands often have dramatic beaches (Harris), wildlife (St Kilda), caves (Staffa), archaeology (Orkney) or churches (Iona), so it is not difficult to understand the appeal of them, simply as interesting places. Many island places would be interesting even if they weren't islands. Several times, however, I have visited a place simply because it is an island. Once or twice I have thought 'This would not be interesting if it was just another bit of mainland – but it isn't and that makes all the difference'.

So, what is the appeal of islands? They are framed and delineated

by the sea. They start and finish in a most definite way, in a way
that a mainland city, county or parish does not. Because of this
they are knowable and quantifiable. They are finite. Islands can be
looked at on the map without the distractions of blurred edges. If
they are small enough they can be visited and walked round in a
day. You can be marooned on a cosy island with a hotel, if you
wish – even if it is only until the first ferry arrives the next day. Or
you can choose even longer and total isolation. You can be alone,
with a tent, for a week and experience true solitude – like Robinson
Crusoe. You can learn a lot about yourself that way.

When is an island not an island? When is an island too small to
be so called? Tradition has it that if it will support a couple of
sheep it's an island, smaller than that and it's just a rock. In his fabulous book, *The Scottish Islands*, Hamish Haswell-Smith uses 40
hectares (about 100 acres) as his cut-off point for inclusion, but
this excludes the wondrous Staffa (33 hectares) and the mighty Bass
Rock (8 hectares), so he had to put those in appendices. The book
catalogues a further 165 islands. There are all manner of defini-
tions – the Vikings required that you be able to sail between an
island and the mainland with your rudder in place – but I prefer to
think that if it *feels* like an island then it is one.

The presence or absence of human habitation imbues an island
with a very distinct aura. The most atmospheric and poignant of all
places are the abandoned villages found in many Scottish islands.
The most famous of these is on St Kilda – evacuated at the request
of the 36 remaining inhabitants in 1930 – but there are many others.
Some of the houses on St Kilda have been restored for use by shep-
herds, naturalists, archaeologists and others. Elsewhere there are
simple piles of rounded stones covered by wind-blown sand and
overgrown with nettles – a sure sign of a one-time human presence.
Very few islands have never been inhabited. The tiny Staffa, North
Rona, the Shiant and Monarch Islands have all had small populations in previous centuries. It is said of the shepherd and his family
on Staffa that they finally decided to leave, about 200 years ago,
when the rattling of the pan on the fireplace, caused by waves
pounding in the caves, became intolerable.

There are around 60 inhabited islands in Scotland, from the biggest
island – Lewis – with a population of around 22,000 to tiny Colonsay
with about 128 people, Fair Isle with 67, Foula with 30 and Papa

Stour with 20. Professor Robin Dunbar at Oxford University has said that around 150 is the ideal number for a human community. There would be enough to perform all the social, commercial and practical functions. One hundred and fifty people can, more or less, be managed by peer pressure, more than that and you need a police force. Everyone knows everyone else.

The small island communities cling on, and even thrive, depending on the quality of the communications with the mainland. In days gone by that meant the islanders' own boats but now we have scheduled (and subsidised) ro-ro ferries, air services, telephones and the internet. On Colonsay, Kevin Byrne owns and operates the House of Lochar – book publisher – almost entirely by electronic communication. He can publish, print and sell books without them ever physically leaving Colonsay, although he does have a bookshop there as well.

The ultimate communication an island can have is a bridge or causeway. Purists argue that an island can't be an island if it has a permanent, rigid link to the mainland. This objection would disqualify Skye for example, the iconic Scottish island in the view of many. Over the years I have been visiting the islands a number have acquired bridges (Skye and Scalpay) or causeways (Berneray and Vatersay) but life as we know it hasn't ended there.

The folk on Vatersay say they never locked their doors before the causeway arrived, but now they do. Even so, crime is still largely unknown on the islands. There is a bus shelter on Shetland, decorated and furnished by the locals, without any fear of vandalism. One acquaintance told me years ago:

> We have no police here but there are a few big lads we can call on if there are any problems – in such cases someone usually ends up being thrown off the pier.

When some drunks from a visiting fishing boat caused problems, late at night, for an island hotel in 2010 they were frightened off by the manager phoning a volunteer fire fighter who drove by with the blue light flashing. Ultimately, however, the long arm of the law will reach out by helicopter or fast boat if necessary, as it did to arrest those fishermen – at 4am.

Sir Winston Churchill had causeways built to connect the southern Orkney islands of South Ronaldsay, Burray, Glims Holm and Lambs Holm to the Orkney Mainland during the Second World War. He did this to create a barrier to protect the Royal Navy, at anchor in Scapa Flow, from German submarines. It worked and the legacy of that building work is that the southern island chain is a thriving part of a vibrant Orcadian community. You can take a short sea passage from John O' Groats to South Ronaldsay and then travel by road, all the way to the Orkney capital of Kirkwall, without getting your feet wet.

For a good part of human history (people have been living on the islands since the end of the last ice age some 10,000 years ago) the sea has been a highway, not a barrier. Even today there are places more easily reached by boat than by road. People lived and worked with the sea, depending on it in a much more intimate way than most of us do today. It should come as no surprise that most ancient settlements, burials and standing stones are close to the water's edge.

In an idle moment I looked at how many sea crossings you would normally need to reach any given island from the Scottish mainland. I came up with one crossing for the likes of Mull, Arran and Barra; two for Iona and Jura; three for Staffa and Noss and yet four for Muckle Flugga, Balta and Uyea (all off Unst in northern Shetland). It seems that two crossings is the maximum number people are prepared to tolerate to get home. Most of the three- and four-crossing isles are now uninhabited. Shetland's Fetlar, at three crossings, clings on but can hardly be said to be thriving.

We should guard against referring to islands as remote places, however. If you live on Papa Westray then it is the centre of the universe to you and Princes Street in Edinburgh seems remote. Fresh vegetable day at the shop (Wednesday) has more importance to you than say late night opening at Marks & Spencer. That new dress is only a click away in any case.

Of all the appealing things about islands, 'sanctuary' is probably the strongest. Britons are island people, after all, and our 'island-ness' has kept us safe on more than one occasion. Every Briton has some idea of what it means to be protected by a channel of water.

When St Columba arrived from Ireland in the sixth century he considered first Oransay and finally Iona on which to establish his sanctuary and centre of Christian teaching. It was always going to be somewhere by the sea, of course, but when you walk through Oransay or Iona today the feeling of sanctuary is heightened by the fact of being on a small island. Fugitives often sought sanctuary on islands, and none more famous than Bonnie Prince Charlie on Skye in 1746 after the Battle of Culloden. Today Scottish islands are sanctuary for wildlife of all kinds. Birds such as the corncrake hold out on Oransay, Coll and Tiree. The Scottish primrose clings to Orkney and the fabulous white-tailed eagle is staging a comeback on Mull.

And the weather? There is no such thing as bad weather – only inadequate clothing. 'Enjoying your holiday?' one lady said to me once. 'How do you know I'm on holiday' I asked. 'Locals don't wear shorts' she said. I go prepared for it to rain every day, all day, but it never does. You tend to get four seasons in a day in Scotland so, if you don't like the weather, just wait 15 minutes. I've had my share of heatwaves too – 15 hours of sunshine every day for a week on more than one occasion. As I sit proof-reading this introduction I've just returned from two solid weeks of T-shirt weather in Orkney.

Actually, it did rain all week once. The sun came out for half an hour on the last day. I was walking along a track, through ancient woods by a loch. The water sparkled in an instant, the tall reed stems in the shallows glowed with an indescribable colour and the sky turned a shade of blue you will not see anywhere else. The woodland birds sang and the skylark took up the chorus from the field opposite. A duck and her brood swam out from their lochside nest, leaving one large and six small, V-shaped, and ever-widening wakes. I wrote in my diary that the trip had been worth it for that half hour. It certainly was, that was 20 years ago and I always think of that moment when I pass the same spot.

I may never discover what it is about islands in general, and Scottish islands in particular, that excites me but they do. Every journey to an island begins with a quickening of the pulse. Each time I look out of my window in March and see the light sparkling on the water, or feel the strength returning to the sun, I know it is time to start checking the ferry schedules.

Richard Clubley 2014

Toy shop, Arran.

CHAPTER 1

Ailsa Craig – A masterclass in island going

'NO RISKS,' SHE SAID. 'If the dog falls over a cliff into a whirlpool, then don't bother coming home'. This was my *'bon voyage'* as I left for island hopping with Col, our young border collie.

We landed on Ailsa Craig, 244 acres of uninhabited rock, nine miles out from Turnberry in Ayrshire. Ailsa rises almost sheer from the beach to 1,100 feet, with a circumference of two miles.

The scene greeting my arrival at Ailsa's rickety pier was one of an industrial wasteland. The only bit of flat ground – a few acres – on the rock is in the east and where the Stevenson lighthouse and quarry were built over a hundred years ago. A narrow gauge railway leads up from the pier head, passing ruined cottages and running into a 'goods yard' 100 yards further on. Points, rusted and overgrown beyond use, direct a spur to the lighthouse. The East Coast Mainline carries on a further half mile or so to the quarry – now just a heap of rubble and rough-hewn boulders of curling stone proportions. The fog horns, gas works and workshop are rusty. Corrugated iron roofs flap in the wind.

The welcome sign on the pier says 'Unsafe – land at your own risk' and the built walkways, their railings storm twisted beyond usefulness, carry more dire warnings. I camped well away from the sheds lest something fall in the night.

I should really have checked the tides before setting off to walk round the beach. I should have looked at a map too and carried plenty of water – but I did none of these. Someone told me low water would be about 10-ish. As to whether it was a spring or neap tide, I was ignorant. I put all this down to holiday excitement, but stupidity might be a better term.

Having passed the: 'Do not pass this notice' notice, traversed crumbling walkways and gained the 'beach', we commenced a tough scramble over car-sized boulders. After an age we walked on a grassy slope for a while before more boulders.

Reptilian shags honked in crevices, the ground was littered with the un-buried dead of the gannet city (pop. 36,000) on the cliffs above. From the sea Ailsa is one of Britain's natural spectacles. Thousands of birds are on impossible slopes, and in the air. Translucent wings against the bright sky. On the beach it is all death.

The sun bore down and we became very thirsty. Col drank from a pool which I thought must be rainwater but wasn't so she had to be restrained. A half full Evian bottle turned out to be contaminated too. Desperation is alarming.

A headland – was it Stranny Point? I hadn't a clue – blocked our path. I thought the tide should fall further but didn't know what was round the corner anyway. We turned back, dreading the boulders, and trying not to dwell on the thirst. Better the devil you know, I thought.

Passing a small cave I noticed green, wet moss in the entrance, and heard the trickling of water. Fine 'rain' was falling from the roof but I couldn't get a good drink. In an earlier bout of stupidity I forgot to pack a whisky tumbler so had bought a plastic one in Girvan. It made no matter because I left the single malt on the mainland anyway, in my haste to the boat.

I now remembered the tumbler was still in my rucksack. It took five minutes to fill in the 'rain' but gave the sweetest drink. I enjoyed 20 minutes worth and Col licked the moss. Homeostasis restored, the walk seemed much easier. The tide had dropped and we missed the big boulders on the way back. The walkways now seemed benign by comparison. In camp I pledged never to be stupid again. If only.

Had there been golfers at Turnberry, on the Ayrshire coast, about 60 million years ago they might have noticed an undersea volcano erupting nine miles offshore. The long since cooled plug from that eruption is now called Ailsa Craig, often referred to by mariners as Paddy's Milestone as it falls half way between Glasgow and Belfast.

The thing that attracted men to Ailsa was the granite. The island is an igneous intrusion. The molten rock from the volcano cooled underground (unlike lava which erupts before solidifying). The 60 million year old intrusion has been exposed by the softer, surface rocks eroding away. The Bass Rock, St Kilda, Rockall and the Flannan Islands were all similarly formed.

Ailsa's granite is of an unusual type – called ailsite – and is perfect for making curling stones. Ailsite is very fine, hard grained granite, producing excellent stones, used all over the world where curling is played. There are Common Ailsa, Blue Hone and Red Hone varieties of which Blue Hone takes the blue riband. Quarry blasting stopped when the island became a bird sanctuary but Kays of Scotland continue to ship a few loose boulders for curling stone manufacture, together with some gift items. Rhona Martin, Fiona MacDonald, Margaret Morton, Janice Rankin and Debbie Knox won curling gold for Great Britain at the 2002 Winter Olympics using Ailsa stones.

Ailsa Craig is also one of the world's most important gannetries. It is home to fewer birds than the Bass Rock, at the mouth of the Firth of Forth, or St Kilda, but Ailsa's 36,000 pairs of gannets is still a lot of guano.

Gannets are stunning birds. They are brilliant and translucent when viewed against a bright sky from the deck of a small boat, rolling on the sea below the vast colony. They have a six foot, black-tipped wing span, black, webbed feet and a beautiful, creamy yellow head. They plunge dive into the sea from a great height to catch fish, their wings folding back at the last minute as they arrow deep after their prey. Their skulls contain shock absorbing material, a bit like bubble-wrap, to cushion the strike at the sea surface.

The northern gannet nests, very sociably, in huge colonies on remote rocky islands and stacks. On Ailsa Craig the top of almost every granite column has a nest or two. Once they have reached breeding maturity, after a few years, each pair will lay a single blue egg per season. They remain faithful to their nest site, returning year after year and so usually meet up, and mate with, their old partner. Chicks generally return to where they hatched to start breeding. The massive increase in gannet numbers on the Bass Rock (6,000 pairs to 40,000 pairs since 1962) is largely due to breeding success on the rock and the return of native chicks.

Gannets can utilise a wide range of prey fish species. They are not fussy eaters. They are also well equipped to range far and wide from the colony and to dive deep after food. They can thus track the shoals and take fish that swim at different depths. This catholic taste means they are less susceptible to vagaries of fish stocks than some other seabirds.

From the sea the colony is an amazing site. Thousands of birds spaced over every available ledge – all keeping just out of stabbing range of their neighbour's fearsome dagger-bill. The constant clamour mingles with the smell of guano which, once sensed, is never forgotten. Thousands more – birds off fishing, returning, just stretching their wings, perhaps, or young 'loafers' without parental responsibility – wheel and soar in the thermal up-draughts where the sea air meets the cliff.

The bird corpses on the beach were things they don't show you in the nature programmes. Professor Sarah Wanless of the Centre for Ecology and Hydrology (CEH), who spent her PhD years squatting in an old granite miner's cottage on Ailsa Craig, told me that the Ailsa gannet cliffs are different from most others in that they have this narrow beach, rather than plunging sheer to the sea, as at St Kilda, Bass Rock and elsewhere, and so dead birds are more evident. Sarah divided her time between counting gannets and rescuing fallen chicks 'that would otherwise be eaten alive by rats'. She hand-reared them at the cottage on mackerel caught off the beach in the evenings. 'One of my chicks made it to Morocco,' she told me.

Gannets are subject to protection under the law on seabirds but the men of Lewis in the Outer Hebrides are licensed to sail to remote An Sgeir every August to harvest 2,000 gannet chicks, or gugas. It is a rite of passage for Lewismen to be invited on the hunt. The gugas, considered a delicacy, are brought back to Ness, pickled and salted, for sale or distribution to friends. Licence returns record 33,690 gugas taken between 1985 and 2001. An Sgeir is one of only three Scottish gannet colonies to suffer a decline in recent years (St Kilda and Ailsa Craig being the other two). The harvest represents about 30 per cent of the annual chick production so it is a prime suspect. Incidentally, there are all manner of recipes and cooking methods for guga. The flavour has been described variously as: salt mackerel-flavoured chicken and kipper with the texture of steak or salt goose. The skin, often eaten separately, 'resembles a dirty dish cloth with the taste of tripe.' For the bachelors of Ness the first guga of the year is said to be the nearest thing to an erotic experience. Kerrs Pink potatoes are the best accompaniment.

I sailed round Ailsa Craig in 2011 with a boatload of tourists. There were 72,000 gannets, sure enough, but it was the puffins that had the visitors squealing with delight and pointing excitedly. Puffins are the most attractive, delightful birds. Often described as 'comic' but I do not hold with that. It is, without doubt, their multi-coloured bill that does it for them. Bold stripes of red blue and yellow adorn the adult bill in the breeding season. There is also a bright orange 'hinge' which assists in the holding of several fishes at once.

Puffins are highly trusting of humans at their breeding sites, in spite of years of persecution for food on St Kilda and elsewhere. I have sat, on still, calm evenings, only a few feet from their burrows in the grassy cliff tops of Fair Isle, Lunga, Mingulay and other such places, watching them come and go with beaks full of sandeels for their single chicks below ground.

Puffins, unlike neighbouring auks such as guillemots and razor-bills, carry several fish at a time back to their chicks waiting in the burrows. The record is 61 sandeels and a rockling in a single beak load. Fish in such large catches are often virtually useless to the chicks however as they are light to the point of transparency. There is a popularly held view that puffins carry multiple catches with heads and tails on alternating sides. The thought being that, as they chase the shoals, they grab alternately to left and right. Not so I'm afraid – the fish are caught and carried randomly.

Since the 1980s puffins at North Sea colonies have suffered, drastically in some years, from crashes in sandeel populations due to over-fishing by humans. Fish prey species have also been affected by sea temperature changes, popularly attributed to global warming although still poorly understood. As oceans warm, the fish move north in search of cooler, more nutrient rich water. In recent years puffins have been seen trying to feed the once scarce pipe fish to their chicks. This is a long, straggly beast, difficult for chicks to swallow and of little food value.

Unlike gannets, guillemots, razorbills and kittiwakes, which nest on highly inaccessible ledges, the puffins lay their eggs in old rabbit burrows or ones they have excavated themselves in grassy cliff tops. This makes them extremely vulnerable to land-based predators such as brown rats. Ailsa Craig once had a teeming puffin colony numbering 300,000 pairs but, after the rats arrived, had been wiped out in about 30 years. Rats easily take eggs and chicks from the burrows. Puffins can live for 20 to 30 years. The adults could escape the rats and return each year to breed but all the eggs or chicks were taken so, once the adults died off through old age or other causes, the colony died.

Rats were first recorded on Ailsa Craig in 1889 – just three years after the lighthouse had been built in 1886 and the two arrivals were probably related according to Bernard Zonfrillo of Glasgow University. Puffins failed to breed there after 1906. There are many unsung heroes in wildlife conservation but Bernard deserves a mention for his determination to see puffins return to the rock. In 1991 he organised the delivery of industrial quantities of rat poison to Ailsa and supervised their eradication. After a lot of waiting, and finger crossing, he recorded the arrival in 2002 of two breeding pairs of puffins. In 2009 there were about 75 pairs, perhaps 300 birds when all the non-breeding juveniles were added in.

I suppose we should spare a thought for the rats. In 1974 hedgehogs were introduced to the islands of North and South Uist, in the Outer Hebrides, to control slugs and snails. Unfortunately this introduction coincided with a decline in the breeding success of internationally important colonies of wading birds. Like the puffins they nest on the ground and their eggs make good convenience food for hedgehogs.

In 2003 an alarmed Scottish National Heritage paid an average of £800 per prickly hog (my Yorkshire grandma used to call them 'Prick-a-back-hodgesons') to have them relocated to mainland sites. The hedgehogs were being killed at first but the rehoming programme was started after public outcry. By 2010 the re-settlement bill had reached £1.2 million, with a further £1 million needed.

The programme has been described as: 'If in doubt, blame the illegal immigrant.' The sad truth is that no one could be certain the hedgehogs' taking of some eggs was entirely to blame for the birds' decline. On North Ronaldsay, Orkney, a similar problem has been, at least in part, attributed to changes in farming practice and climate change. Climate change is becoming everyone's favourite villain. Who knows? In any event there was no such outcry for the brown rats on Ailsa Craig.

What of the future? Perhaps, if the puffins darken the skies around Ailsa with their dense and numberless flocks once again, the tea shop will re-open for the sale of tea towels, mugs, prints and key-rings. Visitors could be offered a tour of the Stevenson lighthouse and climb to the island summit to view Arran, Mull of Kintyre and Ireland. The industrial archaeology could be tidied up into a visitor experience and perhaps Kays of Scotland could sell their souvenir miniature curling stones.

In 2011 the island was for sale at the asking price of £2.5 million. As a business enterprise there'd be a bit of income from the RSPB lease and quarrying operations, but you would still need to sell a lot of tea and tea towels to turn a profit. The market appears to have acknowledged this – the price was slashed to £1.5 million in 2013 and that was still the asking price in March 2014.

Ailsa Craig lighthouse

CHAPTER 2

Great Cumbrae – Nostalgia for sale

IT TOOK ME 50 years to get to Great Cumbrae. When I started island bagging with my trip to Arran, Great Cumbrae didn't seem so attractive. It has no mountains, no great caves, whirlpools or neolithic stone circles. There are no tales of tragic desertion. Bonnie Prince Charlie did not pass through, neither did Robert the Bruce hide here. Cumbrae is not remote or islolated either. You can hop across in ten minutes on the regular car ferry from Largs, which you can reach in an hour by train from Glasgow. There seemed to be very little romance.

Cumbrae is a tiny, green pebble hidden among the larger islands and coastal towns of the Firth of Clyde. For all that it has a strategic position in the great seaway carrying ships from all over the world, in and out of Glasgow – once the second city of the British Empire. Thousands upon thousands of emigrants from Scotland will have slid away to sea on the ebbing tide past Cumbrae. Through the narrow channel between the Cumbraes and Bute, then on past Arran, they have stood on the deck watching their final close up of home. Some will have seen it again, on their return and, perhaps, wept all over again.

Great Cumbrae is not so great, only four miles long by two wide, its highest point is only 417 feet. It gets its name to distinguish it from its even smaller sibling – Little Cumbrae Island – just off shore to the south. Almost every one of the 1,200 or so people that live on Great Cumbrae do so in the island town of Millport, wrapped around Millport Bay at the south end of the island. You wouldn't think it, to drive round the almost empty hinterland, but Cumbrae has the dubious distinction of being the most densely populated of all the Scottish islands. This is a statistical quirk of its small size and proper little town. If you are a lover of peace and quiet you shouldn't be put off visiting.

When I walk along an island pier for the first time there is anticipation of something new and unknown, no matter how much advance reading has been done. In fact, the more research is done ahead of the trip the more questions there will be. What will that beach be like? What will be in the village shop? On uninhabited islands the very ground underfoot is different, according to the season – the ungathered driftwood, the height of the grass, the carpet of thrift or the discarded yet untrampled egg shells. One of the pleasures almost as good as visiting Scottish islands is writing about them. My blank sheet of paper holds the same promise for me. What will I say? What feeling or memory will scream in my head for attention? It is often trivial but, if it is my foremost thought, then it is what I have to say.

On the five-minute bus ride from Cumbrae pier (a bus meets every one of the regular ferries, after its ten-minute crossing from Largs) on this quiet island I had not known what to expect in Millport. Elsewhere 'doon the watter' in the Firth of Clyde there are a few boarded up shops, some peeling paintwork and other signs of both long and short term recession. Millport, surely, must be struggling I thought. How could it possibly be otherwise out here at the end of the line, on the road to nowhere? Then again, how wrong can you be?

Arriving at the eastern end of the town the first view is of the arms of the bay enclosing a clean sandy beach and a couple of tiny islets – the *Eileans*. Slightly further out is Wee Cumbrae – bought in 2009 by a couple of folk wanting to set up a yoga centre.

Between the road and the beach is the promenade and wide, neatly manicured lawns. The Old Tyme swing boats compete for trade with the putting green. Mums and dads have no difficulty in finding a gaily painted red, green, blue or yellow bench from which to watch the sandcastle building and paddling.

The jurassic-looking Crocodile Rock (a natural, crocodilian rock with a painted face) is the most dangerous thing in Millport. Children risk a grazed knee but never a bite. After the beach there are ice-cream, candyfloss and the '60s coffee bar (still with its original red and yellow formica-topped tables and jukebox). As the light fades the coloured bulbs, strung between the lampposts, reflect in the rising tide.

On a sunny day, in the season, the population of this little town can swell to 5,000. Visitors come to remember these simple, innocent pleasures of their childhoods and to let their children taste them. For a few hours Millport provides service with a smile then draws a collective breath as the last ferry leaves and the island is quiet again – until the next day. It was quiet when I arrived and I couldn't work out how the town managed to look so prosperous. 'What are you selling here?' I asked a local. 'Nostalgia,' she said.

Millport developed, not surprisingly, around a mill sited in the town and close to the small harbour during the 18th century. The small town had a magnetic effect on the rural population. Today more than 90 per cent of the population live in and around Millport. Indeed, travelling round the coastal road one gets the impression of there being almost no-one living or working there. When I arrived on the island I had asked someone where I might camp. 'Just drive out of town and camp anywhere,' he said 'You won't disturb anyone, there's no one there.'

In 1634 a revenue cutter was supplied to supervise the collection of import duties and prevent smuggling in the Clyde. A succession of boats – the King's Boat, the Cumbrae Wherry and the Cumbrae Cutter were based at Cumbrae. With whisky at sixpence a pint the profits to be made from smuggling were high and the whole community supported the activity.

Around the start of the 19th century Commander James Crawford of the revenue service leased some land on the Millport seafront from the Marquess of Bute and built himself a very grand house – still the grandest on Cumbrae – called Garrison House. The town developed further around the excise operations based at Garrison House.

Garrison House was leased by Ayr Council during the 20th century but they sought to close it in 1996 as a cost-cutting exercise. The council tried to ship all documents and artefacts relating to Cumbrae across to the mainland but were thwarted by a sit-in of about a dozen locals. After the usual stalemate and political negotiation it was agreed to sell Garrison House to the newly formed Cumbrae Community Development Company, for the princely sum of £100.

Sadly, in 2001, before all the details could be ironed out or planning and development work started, Garrison House was set alight and the interior destroyed. It is thought to have been the work of vandals. Undaunted, the local activists made new plans and applications and eventually succeeded in opening Garrison House to incorporate a medical centre, cafe, museum and some offices. Today it is a very smart building in a prominent position in the town.

Great Cumbrae has survived all the pressures on small island communities that have led to depopulation elsewhere. Re-organisation of councils now means that secondary school children can commute daily to Largs Academy, rather than having to spend a whole week boarding at school in Rothesay on Bute, simply because Cumbrae was once part of Bute. One wonders why arrangements such as this were never managed before.

Faster, more frequent, ferries from Largs to Cumbrae Slip (ten minutes) have replaced the service to Millport Pier (30 minutes). Ro-ro boats with greater car and passenger capacity, and ability to brave almost any weather, have facilitated commuting by workers, as well as the school children. In short, people can live on Cumbrae yet still access and enjoy all the facilities of the mainland. By the same token visitors can get to Cumbrae easily.

These are the factors that make the difference between an island that thrives and one from which the life blood of trade and commerce ebbs away. And yet there is more to it than the simple provision of public services. A small island community has to have enough energetic, forward looking, able people with the determination to make the situation work. One person's protestor might be another person's anarchist – but where would Cumbrae be today had not the small band of locals manned the Garrison House barricades in 1996?

CHAPTER 3

Bute – Victorian holiday resort 'doon the watter'

I MIGHT NOT have given this little corner of Scotland a second glance had it not been for an event 10,000 years ago. The ice that covered northern Britain scoured its way southwards and gouged out two grooves that filled with water when the ice melted. These narrow channels left 30,000 acres of sky, and the land underneath, cut off from the mainland. Sometime after that the land was named Bute, and the channels became known as The Kyles of Bute. Bute began to acquire all the qualities that attract us to such places, its creation was the acceptable face of global warming.

Islands can be republics, kingdoms, owner occupancies or co-operatives but whatever they are we are drawn to them when similar bits of mainland go unnoticed. Islands are defined by the sea. From my regular seat in the Craigmore Pier Café I could see the whole promenade of Bute's capital town Rothesay – a single, horizontal curve round the edge of the bay. The spirit-level sea drew a line on the post-glacial hillside and this is where all the houses have been built. There is a perfect logic to the arrangement making a very practical place to live – the sea at hand for communication and fishing; the town on a single contour making visits to neighbours a leisurely task. I pondered over my pot of tea how silly the town would have looked, strung out round the hill if the sea had not been there.

Bute is a collection of farms, mostly in the south, and rougher, hillier land in the north. It has none of the mountainous grandeur of neighbouring Arran – no spectacular cliffs, whirlpools or cathedral caves. There is neither poignant desertion, remote isolation (the ferry calls 17 times a day) nor magnificent desolation which may be why it has taken me 30 years of island hopping to get here. Bute is a thriving, confident community – away from it all but within quick striking distance of the bright lights. It was worth the wait.

The Victorians came here in their thousands around the turn of the century, and the pilgrimage continued up to the '50s. Glaswegians especially would arrive by paddle steamers, such as the *Waverley*, down the Clyde for one or two weeks of seaside holiday. Looking at archive footage in the Bute Discovery Centre it is hard to imagine where they all slept there were so many. There appeared not to be room on the beaches, insufficient seats on the prom and goodness knows how long the queue for putting must have been. Lucky families (Ma, Pa and the weans) would have a room to themselves, with perhaps even a kitchen. Poorer folk would find an enterprising landlady who had marked out sleeping spaces with chalk on her bedroom floors. The sea front was very different during my visit (although it *was* still only just March). The long sweeping promenades were empty. The seats and shelters were all vacant – waiting for the *Waverley* – but slightly afraid it might never come again. Like almost every other seaside town in Britain, Rothesay began to suffer when the jet package holidays started in the '60s. 'It is cheaper to fly from London to New York than it is to fly to some of the islands,' said one local.

For anyone contemplating a holiday in Bute the Victorian style and splendour of the hotels and guest houses along the front is delightful. Turrets and colonnades and twiddly wrought iron bits on many of the hotels and guest houses make some very inviting frontages. Even as you step off the ferry, perhaps seeking more urgent comfort, the Victorian toilets on the pier are the first tourist attraction. It costs 15p to 'spend a penny' there but the admission charge is well worth it for a look at the original Twyford fireclay urinals, and toilet pans, served by gleaming copper pipes and glass sided automatic cisterns. Sadly the ladies' facility is more modern, having only been added in the 1990s when refurbishments were carried out. It appears the Victorians did not always provide public conveniences for women – most women I know complain there are still never enough. The attendant will escort ladies to view the old fittings in the gents if they are vacant.

Rothesay is a charming, compact little town with all the shops and amenities you might need during your stay. The few narrow shopping streets behind the seafront are paved with slabs and cobbles which always add atmosphere to such places. The prices and style are a bit different from Bond Street or Princes Street, however – '*Lingerie for every size – all bras now £5*' was available at the

Glamour House. There were also a few boarded up units that us dreamers might have rented to see if we could fare any better than the previous tenants. I might have opened a craft, tea or bookshop, perhaps, to see if I could achieve that idyll that so many visitors to the islands dream of.

Early one morning I crossed from St Ninian's Bay on the west coast of Bute with Jock Turner in his small work boat to the tiny off-island of Inchmarnock. The sea was like a mill pond and sparkled brightly, Goat Fell on Arran looked close enough to touch. The three farmhouses on Inchmarnock are all derelict now but the island is home to a herd of highland cattle which Jock and his pal Fram come to tend every day. The cattle eat only the chemical-free grass supplemented by organic silage and turnips grown for the purpose on the island. The heifers are kept to build up the herd and the bulls go for beef – organic Inchmarnock beef.

There were eider ducks and oystercatchers by the shore; a small flock of teal on the wee lochan near the top of the island and hundreds of geese passed overhead in wave upon wave of 'V' formations. The sun was so strong the temptation to lie down and bathe in it was irresistible and during my reverie on the hill top I could hear the eiders calling and the exultant skylarks telling me this surely must be spring. I noted from my watch that it was still only 9.30 on Monday morning and, back at school, my former colleagues would just be trying to interest some 14-year-olds in The National Parks, How to Arrange a Mortgage or Healthy Eating. It was 'tutor time' and I gave silent thanks that I was finally where I had dreamed of being during many tutor times past.

Inchmarnock has a romantic history if one looks, literally, just under the surface. The last of the Vikings brought their wounded here to tend them after King Haakon of Norway was defeated by Alexander III at the Battle of Largs in 1263, a story that gives the fabled raiders a slightly more humane image. I quite enjoyed the thought of some gruff, hairy Olaf gently supporting his friend's head as he took a sip of water.

In 1961 a farmer, ploughing on the hillside where I now sat, scraped the lid off a Bronze Age burial cist and unearthed the complete skeleton of a young woman. She had been about 25 years old when she died and had been buried along with a flint knife and a jet black, lignite necklace. The 135 beads had collapsed in a heap when the animal sinew string rotted but they have been re-assembled and are on display at the Bute Museum, whilst the skeleton was returned to the cist which was closed with a few small slabs. The skull could be seen through a tiny entrance if you knew where to look and, after my eyes adjusted to the gloom in the small hole, I saw The Queen of the Inch gazing up at me.

I was fascinated by this young woman who had died about 3,500 years ago. The knife she was buried with was probably not symbolic, just one of her favourite things perhaps. The burial of it, together with the necklace, showed she had been much loved and respected. The lignite necklaces were produced exclusively in Scotland at that time. A few have turned up in England but they had been carried, not manufactured there – they must have been Scotland's first exports. They appear to resemble amber jewellery from Denmark and gold designs from Ireland. Experts say the beadwork was not of the highest quality but her family clearly gave her the best they could afford and, just as women today, she will have treasured it and loved them for it.

Since my visit, the skeleton has been re-examined using modern archaeological techniques. She has been confirmed as a high status (because bone analysis revealed she ate very little shellfish), local woman. The Queen of the Inch was properly re-interred on the island and will remain undisturbed.

One cannot fully appreciate Bute without considering its proximity to Glasgow, although the trip to the holiday destination 'doon the watter', on the *Waverley* and her sisters from the pier at the Broomielaw may be less common nowadays. A walk along the Broomielaw wharf in the heart of Glasgow can retrace the steps of all those Victorian trippers. The cobble stones are still there, and the huge black mooring bollards, but there is a casino roughly where the ticket office might have stood – so you can gamble without ever travelling to the arcade at Rothesay. Today there is a modern floating pontoon which rises and falls with the tide and is a stop for the local river bus: *Pride of the Clyde*.

The holiday traffic may have fallen off but there is a significant number of travellers in the opposite direction. I caught the seven o'clock ferry out of Rothesay one damp, drizzly morning and joined the 30 or so commuters in the passenger lounge. They were mostly professional types and office workers I guessed – they would have to be at around £2,000 for a boat/train season ticket to Glasgow. 'The journey puts about three hours on your day' someone told me. The early boat didn't seem too traumatic a commitment for the folk, who sat mostly gossiping and analysing the previous evening's football, or topping up their sleep. A few women took the half hour opportunity to do their make-up, and they certainly looked better when they got off than when they got on. It's another 55 minutes to Glasgow on the train but some people keep cars at Wemyss Bay for their onward journey.

I arrived in Glasgow at 8.45 and was swept into the street by the flood of people arriving from all points. I was not heading for work so I turned straight into Starbucks and ordered 'double tall latte and a muffin to stay' ('double tall', because I'm old-school Starbucks). The young chap next to me on the window stools was having a, 'grande skinny cappuccino, room for milk'. Another customer asked, 'Can I get an apple and cinnamon muffin to go?' and a yuppie, talking earnestly to his boss, used the expression, 'business team' ten times at least. I mention all this because I'd breakfasted in Bute two hours earlier, and would be back there for tea – narrow lanes to the fast lane in no time at all. In Chile you can ski in the mountains in the morning and sunbathe on the beach in the afternoon – this felt a bit like that.

In Britain we are quite used to the availability of castles and grand houses to visit, but it comes as quite a shock when we find one in a seemingly out-of-the way place. St Magnus Cathedral in Kirkwall, Kinloch Castle on Rum and, I suppose, St Columba's Abbey on Iona are all treasures that, apart from their other functions, are testament to an ancient commitment to the little places. The red sandstone gothic palace of Mount Stuart, five miles south of Rothesay, must be one of the most stunning examples of island architecture, even including the three examples above.

John Crichton-Stuart, third marquess of Bute has been described as 'the best non-professional architect of his generation'. Together with architect Sir Robert Rowand Anderson he planned and built the present Mount Stuart on the ashes of the old one during the last two decades of the 19th century. When the marquess died in 1900 the house was still unfinished but the fourth incumbent, also John Crichton-Stuart, had less interest in the house and the finishing touches were never made (a bit like my own DIY projects). Although the present marquess, Johnny Bute, is getting on with a few jobs today.

Mount Stuart is the finest example of the gothic revival style in Scotland. The view of the house as I approached down the wooded drive, carpeted with snowdrops, was stunning. The house is closed in the winter but I was allowed a sneak tour. Coloured marble and granite columns; stained glass with prisms inset to scatter rainbows onto the marble; immense tapestries and fine furniture. Mount Stuart was the first house in Scotland to be lit by electricity and the first anywhere with a heated indoor swimming pool. After that the grand dining room, billiard room and bedrooms seemed almost commonplace – almost but not quite. My guide saved until last the magnificent marble chapel, the size of a small church and flooded with light through the ruby red stained glass and reflected off the white marble.

The Rothesay Pavilion, an art deco listed building built in 1938, continues to provide year round entertainment for locals and visitors. Money is needed for a face lift but inside there was the smell of fresh paint, the gleam of polished floors and the delighted screams of the Senior Citizens Curling Club. I saw them through the window towards the climax of this keenly fought contest (I think it was a grudge match and blues were just shading it from the reds). I couldn't understand why they were not using the famous sweeping brushes but then I realised this was carpet curling – well lino curling actually – and the stones were on wheels. The referee was a Community Outreach Worker for the Isle of Bute Community Support Network and she was responsible for the collecting, transporting and seeing safely home again of the players. She was a bubbly enthusiast for what she is doing and was quick to list all the other regular and occasional events in the Pavilion. The curlers may have been less supple than Rhona Martin and her Olympic team but they all had a twinkle in the eye and a confidence, determination and humour that age had not wearied.

The five mile jaunt from Rothesay, north to Rubodach, is a pleasant outing and qualifies in my *Book of Pleasant Outings* as a four star entry by virtue of the excellent opportunity for tea and cakes at the end of it. The Colintraive Hotel is reached by the five minute ferry crossing of the Kyle which is at its narrowest here, just a few hundred yards. The hotel was built in 1850 as a hunting lodge for The Marquess of Bute. It was taken over in 2003 by Patricia Watt and has since been picked out by The Good Hotel Guide as one of the very best in Scotland for good food and service at affordable prices. Patricia told me that she has recently opened a village shop and post office next door which provides an excellent service to the locals. 'There are lots of talented people in the village: knitters, artists, aromatherapists and the like. The shop gives them a window for their goods and services, as well as being a meeting point for a chat when they buy their copy of *The Buteman* or the *Herald*.' Since my visit, Patricia has added a Heritage Centre, Sculpture Park and Community Garden. 'We try to support the local community and businesses by being open and providing fresh produce every day throughout the year,' she told me.

Today Bute is facing all the issues of the 21st century. There is modern economic development at the Bute Enterprise Park for instance, housing Fine Foods, Flexible Technology, Photography, Historic Scotland and The Coastguard. There is a vacant unit and, once again, I got to pondering what use I could put it to. It would have to something forward looking I thought. *The Buteman* was providing a forum for island debate about wind farms, fish farms and recycling; as well as coverage of ploughing matches and sponsored swims.

The title: 'Gateway to the Isles' is often awarded to Oban further north, but there's a side gate too – over to Rothesay then north through Colintraive to Kintyre. From there you can cross to Islay, Jura, Colonsay and onwards to Oban and beyond. Didn't that glacier do well?

CHAPTER 4

Eigg and Gigha
– Owning your own island

EIGG, A MEMBER OF the small isles between Mull and Skye, is a well wooded Hebridean island about four miles by six. The small population practices the island industries of farming and tourism.

I was visiting Eigg in 1987, and had wandered down to the pier on my last day to check the departure time for the Caledonian MacBrayne ferry. In the days before the ro-ro service we had hove-to out at sea and clambered down a gangway in to a flit boat to be brought ashore on arrival, and the reverse would be true for departure.

'Don't speak to me of Caledonian MacBrayne,' said the middle-aged man in the shabby tweeds, who I had met on the road. 'That organisation is a useless, socialist, drain on hard earned taxes. It brings absolutely no benefits to the island whatsoever.'

'Never mind the politics,' I said. 'Just tell me the ferry time.'

'You can't have the time without hearing the politics first. Who are you anyway?' he said. I told him.

'Bloody tourist. CalMac ships dozens of you bloody fellows out here, and for what? You don't spend anything when you get here'. He seemed not to realise there was nothing much to spend money on and was gesticulating wildly by this point.

'Visitors drop almost as much litter as the locals,' he went on. 'The local bucks buy cases of beer from the post office then sit in their Land Rovers, drinking and throwing the empties out of the window. The other day I collected hundreds and lined them all up along the centre of the road to make a point – it'll all be to no avail.'

'You sound as if you own the place,' I said.

'I do actually, the name's Schellenberg, I own the whole island for what good it does me,' he said. 'The ferry leaves at 12 o'clock,' he added and walked off.

My attention was drawn to a sleek, expensive looking yacht that had entered the bay. I could hear the rattle of the anchor chain paying out from where I was stood, overlooking the pier. 'That's Suki Schellenberg – the laird's wife,' someone said. 'It's another world, innit pal,' he added.

Keith Schellenberg is well remembered on Eigg, not always fondly. The larger than life character had a very colourful career before buying Eigg in 1975, after falling in love with islands on his Hebridean yachting adventures. Schellenberg's family were originally from Liechtenstein but he was born in Yorkshire in 1930. He was a businessman; captained Yorkshire at Rugby; a member of the British Olympic bobsleigh team; a racer of antique Bentley's and a sailor. In 1980 Schellenberg married Suki, daughter of Major-General R.E. Urquhart, who had commanded the British forces at the Battle of Arnhem during the Second World War.

Keith Schellenberg aspired to the life of a Highland laird. There is a lovely house on Eigg – The Lodge – completed in 1927 and boasting 12 bedrooms and palm trees in the garden but this was the late 20th century and times had changed. Schellenberg's nostalgia for the 1920s did not chime with the ambitions of his islander tenants – or even with their modest desires for roofs that didn't leak.

The laird wanted to turn the island into a nature reserve, ban shooting and most fishing. He wanted to attract more people but made the same mistake that has been made elsewhere – he openly advertised and didn't check out the credentials of incomers. Some that came did very well but hippies were also attracted to what they thought would be a life style of dropping out and turning on. Island life *can* be idyllic but mostly it is very tough. The weather, the isolation, especially in winter, the cost of shipping and the gold-fish bowl existence are not for everyone. Cracks began to appear.

At the time of my first visit to Eigg, in 1987, it still existed in that 1950s time-warp of wrinkly tin roofs, a shop with not much stock and outside toilets. I was looking for 'the Tea and Craft Shop' one day and, walking up the track of what I thought was the right place, passed a girl of about ten sitting on a toilet bucket in a sentry box with no door. Squares of newsprint hung on a nail on the wall.

There was no wash hand basin available but that did not stop the lass running up the drive after me to help her mum serve the tea and chocolate cake. Hector MacLean, who had been doctor on Eigg since 1951, reported the most common ailment to be 'The

Eigg bug' also known as 'The Bomb'. The Eigg bug takes the form of diarrhoea and vomiting.

Maggie Fyffe moved from Bolton to Eigg in 1975, just after Keith Schellenberg bought the place. She was attracted there by one of his adverts and has survived everything since then. She is currently secretary of the Isle of Eigg Trust.

The islanders at that time were suffering under the worst kind of 'landlordism'. Money was being taken out of the island in the form of rent but nothing was being spent on maintenance. In 1988 Margaret Williams, Schellenberg's estranged wife who owned half of Eigg, realised that the disrepair was lowering the value of her investment so took her ex- to court to force a sale. After years of wrangling, the court found in her favour but salvation for Eigg was still a long way off. In 1992 Schellenberg bought her out which solved Margaret's problem but plunged Eigg back into the same mess it had always been in.

Outright hostility between the Eigg folk and their landlord was becoming more evident. In 1994, in the dead of night, a mysterious fire broke out which destroyed Mr Schellenberg's vintage Rolls Royce. The laird blamed the locals and relationships deteriorated further. They were no longer prepared to be afraid of summary evictions – how much worse could it get anyway?

The Isle of Eigg Trust, which had been formed in 1991, started to appeal for funds and they flooded in. In 1995 the islanders were beaten to their plan to own the island by a quick, secret sale to a mysterious German artist, called Maruma, for £1.6 million. Maruma's purchase turned out to be fraudulent, however, and the island fell into the hands of a Hong Kong businessman – Hans-Rainer Erhardt. Back on the market, this time for £2million, the Eigg Trust jumped in with a bid of £1.2million, made possible by an anonymous donation of £750,000. On 12 June 1997 the islanders got their island and the mother of all parties began.

Eigg has just celebrated again. In June 2012 it was their 15th birthday but I wasn't able to attend the party. I was able to go, however, to Gigha, 100 or so miles to the south. Gigha had celebrated ten years of community ownership in March 2012. I went in June and had a good chat with a few locals to see how things had gone since their buy-out.

In 2002 Gigha had been suffering much as Eigg had done.

There had been four landlords in 12 years, all with different agendas. The policy of spend nothing and draw rents, familiar on Eigg, was practiced on Gigha. One landlord had even told a friend: 'You can make money here as long as you don't spend anything'.

The population was down to 95 with not enough children in the school for a game of 5-a-side football. The shop and hotel were under threat and people wanted out. The hotel was owned by the laird and he wouldn't allow locals (in tied cottages) to offer B&B as it would compete with the hotel.

The Giogheans would have accepted a 'benevolent despot'. They weren't opposed to the idea of a landlord, they just wanted one who would care about them. In fact a benevolent landlord might have been the majority preference, there was no strong political drive for land reform at that time.

Malcolm Potier had been the last landlord before the buy-out and, just like Maruma on Eigg, had allegedly used someone else's money for the purchase. The island was double-mortgaged and, with Potier locked up in Australia for, allegedly, ordering a contract killing of his former girlfriend – because she, allegedly, denied him access to his daughter. The island fell to a Swiss bank, who sold it to Mr Holt of Leisure Parks. (Sound familiar?)

When the Isle of Gigha Heritage Trust took over ownership of the island in 2002 there was another great party. The islanders were thrilled but some didn't quite grasp the concept. One or two turned up at the hotel bar that night expecting free drinks because: 'We own the pub now, don't we?'

The heady expectations of that crazy night soon met a cooler dawn of reality and folk got on with the hard work of re-building their island. A lot of people, especially young families, who had left in frustration, now returned to Gigha. The average age of the population fell and everyone was offered the chance to buy a plot of land and these sales funded the refurbishment of existing houses.

Achamore House – the 'big house' that had been built by Colonel Horlicks, a former owner of Gigha and famous for his bed-time drink – was sold off by the trust to help repay a £1.25 million chunk of buy-out money. The house is now privately owned and run as a B&B (although, in 2013, it was on the market again at around £800,000) but the extensive gardens are community owned (sorry, I mean Community Owned) and open to the public to raise further funds. Everywhere you go on Gigha you will see signs for 'The Community Owned...'. They are very proud of their island and what they have achieved in the (then) biggest community buy-out in British history.

Community Owned camping facilities are available near the pier but I'd been used to wild camping the previous week and the one other tent there made it feel crowded so I moved on. Four miles north, at the end of the road, there was absolute peace and quiet. I pitched my tent on the grass above the beach and looked out over Knapdale on the mainland and the islands of Jura and Islay in the north and west. Islay's new ferry – MV *Finlaggan* – passed a few miles away doing 16 knots and 20 minutes later a gentle ripple from her bow wave made a lovely sound as it washed up my small pebble beach.

I swam in a blue sea under a blue sky and laid out on the short grass to air-dry in the sun – it was June and island-going seldom gets better than that. After a super bar meal and some good craic in the Community Owned Gigha Hotel I found my way back to the tent by the last of the sun (there is little darkness at this latitude at that time of year) only to be kept awake by the noisy neighbours. The screeching oyster catchers are my favourite bird and they can disturb me anytime they want. They did pipe down long enough, however, for me to enjoy the corncrake males rasping from the long grass. In weather like this I often prefer a tent to a B&B or hotel for the very reason that you get closer to some truly wonderful sounds. During the short darkness there were more ripples on the beach as a ship passed by in the night

Next day I went to the annual fundraiser in the Community Owned Village Hall. I guessed at the weight of a halibut (wrongly), had a go on the coconut shy and guessed the sweets in a jar (again without success). There are 23 children in the school now, against the 4 at take over. Behind the stalls youngsters were confidently learning about the responsibilities that will one day be theirs. There is less of a generation gap on small Scottish islands. All ages are needed to pull together to make anything work, whether it be dancing, football or fundraising.

The football pitch, incidentally, is behind the hall and, despite having recently been cut for hay, was the venue for the annual challenge match against a team from Norfolk. Sadly this had to be stopped following a serious injury to one of the players, who was taken away by helicopter. The match was formally abandoned, eventually, at about ten o'clock that night, when the referee reached across the hotel bar to pick up his pint and realised his stop watch was still running.

The 15 March 2012 was Gigha Day. The island was bursting at the seams for the tenth anniversary celebrations. Every available bed was taken and the ferry worked overtime to carry revellers from the mainland.

The school children (now enough for 11-a-side) had been working hard to raise celebration funds – their Isle of Gigha Tenth Anniversary mugs sold well. Mums and dads held Race Nights, Quiz Nights and Roll-a-pound-at-a-whisky-bottle nights in the hotel to add to the fund. They made enough to book folk bands: *Trail West* and *Macadam* for the ceilidh to end all ceilidhs. The *Campletown Junior Pipe Band* visited; Elaine Duffus wrote a song; speeches were made (Jim Hunter told anyone who still thinks the buy-out had been expensive that it cost the same as 60 yards of the Edinburgh tramway) and a commemorative stone and plaque were unveiled.

The stone, formerly used for shaping iron cartwheel rims, had lain overgrown and forgotten, so they picked it up and gave it pride of place. Gigha's heritage is being dusted off, alongside all the new technology. What is it about islanders and their standing stones? John Martin hoisted the Gigha flag, assisted by the three youngest children. Screen Machine – a cinema in a lorry – came for the day and showed a double bill of War Horse and a documentary about the buy-out.

In the 12 years since the Isle of Gigha Heritage Trust took the island into local ownership they have gone from strength to strength. The wind turbines now sell power to the National Grid to pay for housing refurbishment. A fourth turbine arrived in 2013. There will also be a battery – as big as the village hall, apparently, to store energy on windy days, for use on non-windy days. There may even be a charging point for electric cars. The shop, hotel and grand gardens are all part of the enterprise too.

Henri Macaulay runs a craft shop and gallery in buildings built by Argyll and the Isles Enterprise in 2004 – part of their contribution in support of the community. Leading Scottish artists have exhibited here, including John Lowrie Morrison in 2011 and Ernie

Upton in 2012. You can also join Henri for stained glass making or Gaelic music workshops.

'The ceilidh was great,' Henri told me, 'everyone pitched in to make the best buffet you ever saw and then we danced it off, starting with a strip-the-willow lasting half an hour.' It was light when the last revellers left to walk along the road to the village.

During the evening news came through that Samantha Durnin, aged ten on the original Gigha Day, had been safely delivered of Taylor. One of the strengths of small island communities is the togetherness of the generations. I wouldn't bet against Taylor hoisting the flag in 2022.

There is a lot of work still to be done on Gigha, as there is on Eigg. With small populations and limited resources there are plenty of projects to fill several lifetimes. Three second-hand wind turbines on Gigha are bringing in money. They are called Faith, Hope and Charity – and the islanders have enough of these qualities to convince me their island is in good hands.

'So long as we all keep rowing in the same direction,' said one.

In April 2013 consultation began over the future of Raasay, east of Skye. The 200 residents were asked by the Scottish government to consider a community buyout, to resolve the future of the sporting rights and other issues on the island. The community did take over control of the shop but shopkeeper, Jane, told me in 2014 the islanders have decided, for now, not to take things any further.

Flower-filled wellies, Gigha Primary School.

CHAPTER 5

Islay – A special kind of freedom

SCHOOL TEACHING IS A high pressure way of life. It is a life regulated by bells, terms and calendars. Breaks, be they long or short, are taken by the clock. During lessons one may not visit the toilet without first calling for someone to hold the fort. When the bell sounds at the end of a period a teacher may have to choose between a quick trip to the loo or a coffee – there often not being time for both. When the bell rings for the next session it is: 'seconds out, round two, ready or not.'

In school there had been two or three of us who shared a passion for Scottish islands. Talking about islands became like a therapy for us – a ready escape in a few moments at lunchtime. It was our default setting whenever we came together, like football is for others. We would use islands to take our minds off the most recent difficult child, examination failure or summons to the head's office. Not exactly the opiate of the masses, but Scottish islands became the calming drug of choice for a small, select band in the school.

My pal, Steve, and I would sit, on an unseasonably warm February or March day, with bright, early year sunshine sparkling in a puddle outside the staffroom window. It would put us in mind of that incredible effect the spring sunshine has on the Atlantic when viewed from an island cliff top. The sparkling blue and white sear into the brain and the new strength of the sun gives a tan to the face and hands that will last all summer. 'Where have you been, Scotland again I suppose?' they always asked when I got back to school after Easter. 'You look well – it rained in the Dordogne.'

A young, student teacher once overheard Steve and me talking about St Kilda. 'Ooo, have you been to St Kilda?' she asked. 'I've always wanted to go there. I've been as far as Harris and Lewis but no further.' Caroline would have been attractive enough without the island visits in her CV but our interests were further aroused when she started to wax lyrical about the Shiant Isles. She slid across the three, plastic covered chairs to join us.

'No, Caroline, don't do it.' Mike, who was not noted for his concern for young teachers' virtue, begged her not to join us. 'They will bore you to death with island talk,' he said, but it was too late. Caroline answered our searching questions about abandoned islands, community buy-outs, ferry routes and gave the pros and cons for bridges and causeways – she was voted unanimously into the club. Caroline took part in many discussions that summer before she had to go back to college. I don't know what became of her but I just know she will have done well. She went armed with a passion and an ability to imagine the remote places when pressure builds up at school.

Nigel Laybourne is from a different mould altogether. A tall, slim, tough character with a beard, and about our own age, he needed no-one's permission to park wherever he wished in the staff room. Long and dedicated service had earned him that. He would sit with his Tupperware box of sandwiches and hold court on how to diagnose carburettor problems in a Triumph TR6, or ponder out loud how someone might get sufficient hydrostatic head in a new loft conversion. He was a technology teacher.

Nigel is a doer and a fixer. He was also Head of Year for the cohort of children I found myself attached to for most of my time at the school. Nigel's assemblies were legend. He could hold 350, testosterone charged and oestrogen soaked teenagers in rapt attention with illustrated talks on subjects such as: '*My Balls of Steel – How I ruined my hips kayaking round Greenland and had to have them replaced.*' He retired in 2009.

Nigel was a kayak instructor in his spare time and every Friday would nip across to the swimming pool at lunchtime to teach a loyal band of children about Eskimo rolls and self-rescue. Such free giving of time is one of the things that mark special teachers out from the rest. He first sat in a kayak, aged 15, on Lake Bala in Wales and by age 25 was a senior instructor. By 30 he had qualified as an international sea kayak coach. Nigel helped found the Sheffield Education Canoe Association and he spent many summers in Holland teaching European families to paddle. He had been invited to teach in the Netherlands after they moved to sea kayaking from inland waterways and found it dangerous.

Mr Laybourne would make guest appearances at our island meetings from time to time. 'I've kayaked round there,' he would say, in reference to the island or archipelago under discussion, adding: 'We had to shelter in a cave for three days' or: 'We landed for lunch and got chased by starving chickens; shouted at by the Laird or caught in a deer stampede.' Islay, in the Inner Hebrides, was the focus of one particular lunchtime seminar. We pulled our seats into a circle, threw another chair leg into the staffroom stove and refilled the kettle as Nigel began:

'We put our boats (there were four of us) into the water on the mainland, opposite the island of Gigha, and paddled round the south end of that island, across to Ard Imersay on Islay. It was about 12 miles, across open water, and far enough for a first day. It was late May and we camped on the dunes. The *machair* flowers – daisies, lady's fingers and orchids – were fabulous and corncrakes called from the irises. We don't go to these places for tourism, or to meet the locals, but our camp site was only a two-mile walk along the shore of a sea loch to Ardbeg distillery, so we made an exception. Islay is the capital of islands whisky making, one could easily paddle to distillaries at Laphroaig, Caol Isla, Lagavulin, Bowmore, Port Charlotte, Bunnahabhain and the others but when you've seen one mash tun you've seen them all.'

When Nigel got to this point in his narrative, teachers being teachers, we had to go round the group to give everyone a chance to show how much they knew about single malts. Pretty soon the whole staff room was joining in. The ladies, of course, didn't know how we could drink the stuff because it tasted of diesel oil and cough medicine. All the old clichés came out such as 'acquired taste'; 'water of life' and 'only for medicinal purposes'.

I was teetotal until, aged 56, I visited Highland Park distillery in Orkney one wet Sunday afternoon. I had been building up to breaking the life-long pledge for some time. Being a lover of Scottish islands, and constantly hearing about whisky, I decided to find out what all the fuss was about. I took my two wee drams of Highland Park – a 12-year and a 16-year. I could tell the older one was smoother but apart from that the Earth didn't move. Ah well – acquired taste I thought. I've since grown to find the Islay malts quite palatable but generally haven't enjoyed the blended whiskies. My wife says I have expensive tastes. Whisky doesn't seem to do much for me. Perhaps I'm not drinking enough.

There is an image and mystique built up around single malt whisky. In their advertising the good folk at Ardbeg describe Islay as:

'a remote, antique land – a wild and untamed place where Celtic monks found refuge from raiding Norsemen.' I'm surprised by some of this. If I've ever made the mistake of calling an island 'remote' the locals have been quick to say 'remote from where? London may be the centre of *your* world but yon's the place that feels remote tae us, not this island.' They're happy enough to call it remote when it suits them.

Then there's all the stuff about soft water, fertile soil and peat. Ardbeg is described as the peatiest and smokiest of all Islay malts (the claim is also made for Laphroaig). 'It is peat – that soggy, unassuming matter which gives Ardbeg its flavour'. Now I can just about go along with that, but where did the advertising writers get:

> an explosion of crackling peat sets off millions of flavour explosions on the tongue. The peat effervesces with tangy lemon and lime juice, black pepper pops with sizzling cinnamon spiced toffee. This is followed by a wave of brine infused with smooth buttermilk, ripe bananas and currants. Smoke gradually wells up on the palate bringing a mouthful of warm creamy cappuccino and toasted marshmallows. As the taste lengthens and deepens, dry espresso, liquorice root and tarry smoke develop, coating the palate with chewy peat oils...?

I tried adding lemon, lime, pepper, cinnamon, toffee, buttermilk, salt water, bananas, currants, marshmallows and liquorice to my 'cappuccino' but the effect was not good. Perhaps the bananas weren't ripe enough.

Finally on the subject of whisky, I wonder who has £10,000 to spend on a leather case with two (yes, just two) bottles of whisky in it. To be fair the leather gun case is *'lovingly hand stitched'* and does contain eight solid silver whisky tumblers, an engraved pen and a couple of books. This offer by Ardbeg is limited to 250 worldwide. I wonder if anyone ever buys this sort of stuff, or if the offer is more about seeking to create an exclusive, luxury image of a particular type. If I won £101,000,000 on the lottery (as one couple near where I live did recently) would I, even then, really go out and buy a leather case containing two bottles of booze? I write this on the day in 2012 when the Scottish government has introduced a legal minimum price for a unit of alcohol of 50p.

'Shut up, Clubbers,' someone said 'Let Nigel finish his story'.

'Next day we rounded the headland at Mull of Oa and hauled

out at the end of the afternoon on a beach where a pretty burn, Abhainn Ghil, ran down to the sea. Such places are inaccessible to all but paddlers and hardy walkers so we usually have them to ourselves. There was plenty of sun-bleached driftwood for a good fire so we cooked our rice and explored the remains of old black houses and a chapel before bed. Our beach was west facing. There was a sunset of the type island dweller, writer and artist – Mairi Hedderwick – calls soul-searing and just enough movement in the sea for ripples from the Gulf of Mexico to make a gentle sound on the shell-sand beach.

The next leg was round Rhinns Point to Kilchiarran Bay, across the wide mouth of Loch Indaal. The route took us between Portnahavan and the tiny, rocky islets of Orsay and Frenchmen's Rock. It was an exposed day, mostly, but this short passage at around lunchtime brought us close in-shore to the cosy little hotel bar at An Tigh Seinnse.

Passing a few rocks, just offshore, we noticed seals hauled out and enjoying the sun. The sea was almost flat calm and we glided silently towards them, only inches from the rock. I startled one and it and it rolled off the rock, flopping straight onto the deck. We looked at each other for a second – I smelled its fishy breath before it plopped into the water with a single wriggle.

The boat brought us close to lots of wildlife. Some days, dolphins would follow us from morning until night. We were kindred spirits, sharing the ocean and each no threat to the other. Navigating along the bases of soaring sea cliffs we would see vastly overcrowded, slum tenements of sea birds. With sometimes hundreds of thousands of birds the cawing, cackling sounds and fishy smells would be enough to navigate by in thick mist. Fishermen of old often did that. There'd be puffins on the grassy slopes at the top, or gannets. More gannets on the ledges, cheek by jowl with fulmars, razorbills, guillemots and kittiwakes. At the bottom, among the boulders, there may be the archaeopteryx-like shags – deep throated honking echoing in caves and sounding like the end of the world.

If the birds were startled they would pour down to the sea like a katabatic wind – puffins and guillemots paddling across the deck of the kayaks if we happened to be in their flight paths. Birds were our constant companions. There might be the odd golden eagle soaring, or a fulmar spitting oily, smelly deterrent at us if we walked too close to a nest during an evening stroll. Of them all though my favourite was the piping, screeching oystercatcher as we fell asleep in our tents and again to wake us in the morning.

It was very pleasant sitting on proper chairs, in the sun at An Tigh Siennse, and enjoying a good lunch without having to prepare it ourselves. A dram of Ardbeg slipped down well. Luxury and indulgence are always heightened and appreciated after physical effort to get to them. It was still only late May but the sun burnt through the clear air onto our faces. People who complain about Scotland's weather often don't realise that when it's good it's brilliant. I looked at my hands – the salt water had cleaned every last trace of school workshop swarf from the pores. They looked bleached, like driftwood, on the palms and a deep tan was developing on the backs.

I spoke too soon. Dawn at Kilchiarran Bay brought a sea change. Grey, lumpy rollers; grey, leaden skies and a cold wind. Even the grass had lost its greenness. It was a day for rolling over and going back to sleep but someone said we should get moving and have the wind behind us for a while.

Kilichiarran had been lovely on the previous evening but it's an awful place in the cold and driven rain. All colour and perspective had drained from the land and seascape. Our gear was cold and wet to the touch and not at all pleasant to pack and stow.

We paddled north east along the coast, keeping our heads down and, apart from concentrating on staying up-right and navigating, we thought only of getting somewhere and stopping again. In the end the campsite chose us rather than the other way round. The wind had freshened during the day and we reckoned it was blowing force seven or eight by the time we half crashed, half paddled onto a most unsuitable boulder beach at Port Domhnuill Chruinn – about three miles short of Islay's north east corner at Rubh a Mhail. Kayakers are like fishermen, winds are always stronger and waves are always higher, just as fish are always bigger than actually, but it was a very blowy day for all that.

We dragged ourselves up the beach to find a dry cave offering shelter, of sorts, from the gale. Had it not been for our boats we would have been cut off in this most inhospitable spot. The cliff above was an unclimbable overhang and outcrops at either end of the beach were impassable – even as the tide fell. When we turned to look at the angry sea again we realised we were indeed cut off, kayaks or no kayaks.

In situations like this it's not so bad at first. There's plenty to do securing the boats; organising the best possible pitches for the tents and cooking food. Morale was high. The storm will have blown over by morning, we thought, and we'd be away. There was a good supply of dry wood in the cave so a campfire was organised to warm us all up before bed.

In camp we would each do our own cooking. A big part of our several motivations for being on those trips was solitude and the private, independent challenging of ourselves to be self-contained, both physically and spiritually. In some ways I might have preferred to go alone but sea kayaking is too dangerous for that. Even so we could still retreat into our own little worlds at times. The first challenge was to buy and stow enough of the right kind of food for the entire trip. We could have got fresh supplies in a few places around Islay but I don't think we ever bought much more than an ice cream. Food had to be long life, energy giving and keep us regular. One cannot afford either form of bowel upset when sitting in a boat all day. If sea conditions were too difficult to land we sometimes had to stay afloat for 20 hours. At such times comfort breaks involved wedging one's self between two kayaks and having them kept as steady as possible by a discreet and sympathetic partner.

Porridge with dried fruit was for breakfast most days. I did like to start the trip with a full Scottish for a couple of mornings but the phaff was a novelty that soon wore off when trying to wash up in a cold burn. You can't have fresh sausages much beyond two days anyway. Cod and mackerel were readily available in summer months so we sometimes trolled a line behind the boats to catch a bit of variety for supper. I usually found room in the boat for a fruit cake in a tin as I was often paddling on my birthday and it made a nice treat.

After three days and nights in the cave, and no sign of the wind abating, morale was not so high. We had taken one, tatty paperback each and these had been long since passed round. We found a natural shelf cut into the cave wall, high and dry at the back and left the books there for the next castaways. They were secured in place by two stone bookends, shaped a little like Lewis Chessmen. Whoever joined the Port Domhnuill Library next would find the opening hours convenient and the non-existent system of fines to their liking. They'd be happy so long as they liked John Grisham and Harry Potter or had the ambition to learn Spanish in a weekend. Food, fuel and drift wood had run out – there had been no camp fire the previous evening. No one else knew where we were, mobile phone signals were non-existent and the end of the school holiday was fast approaching'.

Someone in the staff-room audience commented that the Head of English had once missed a flight back from Florence at the end of a half-term holiday and been docked pay. We all understood the need to get those kayaks back in the water but the waves were still massive. In any event the bell was summoning us to afternoon lessons so we had to leave Nigel and friends in the cave a little longer. As it happened Steve and Nigel both had free periods (called non-contact periods in the new politic-speak, to disabuse colleagues of any thought of relaxation). Nevertheless Nigel was asked not to continue with the yarn until we could next foregather in that place. At the end of school, a few days later, Nigel went on...

'On the morning of the fourth day in the cave we decided we had to make a break out. The sea was still up but frustration was making us brave. The most dangerous bit in a sea such as this is the first few feet – where you might be dashed back on the rocks (much as with sky diving, the dangerous bit is the last foot). By standing in the water three of us could steady the first kayak and give a power assisted launch at a suitable gap in the wave train.

Hans shot out into the sea, somehow through, or over, the first wave and was gone. There were two of us left to launch the second boat in the same manner; I helped the third kayak and was then alone to launch myself. We had done it in this order as mine was the heavier and sturdier boat and could be wriggled off the rocks – seal-fashion.

My boat was a customised version of a Nordkap, made for me by Valley Canoes of Nottingham. A sealed bulkhead had been placed just in front of my feet and the rear bulkhead moved a foot back to leave space behind my seat for lunch and a few essentials. Access to the forward and aft watertight holds was through seals on the decks and that's where all the supplies went. I also had a little cradle between my knees for a coffee flask if it became necessary to have lunch afloat, as it sometimes did. It was essential to take in some liquid during the day to prevent cramps but one couldn't drink too much on the water, of course, to reduce the need for the toilet.

I paddled for my life through the first few waves, straight out to sea. I kept going, pushing as hard as I could to get clear of the rocks. I had no idea whether any of the others had made it because as soon as each boat cleared our little headland it was carried swiftly up the coast by wind, and tide. Fortunately it was going in the right direction.

In spite of my fear it was good to be back on the water and to feel I was doing something about the situation. After a nervous hour I made it round the headland and into the Sound of Islay. The wind and waves were still considerable but now they were coming from a different direction – funnelling straight up the narrowing sound into my face.

The land was closing in on both sides – Islay on my right and Jura to the left. Through the claggy weather I could see other kayakers battling the conditions off the Jura shore. There appeared to be seven or eight of them, but no sign of my pals. The sound narrowed further and I began to relax. There is something comforting about the proximity of land. It feels safer, even if the land is the true hazard for a flimsy Kayak.

After some further hours of paddling I made it to the ferry terminal at Port Askaig. All of a sudden, in the lee of the shore, everything fell still. The kayak glided the last few feet to a gentle crunch on the gravel bottom. A small crowd gathered to say: 'Are you OK? Your friends are all here.'

I was so exhausted I couldn't move. I didn't have the strength to climb out. Someone handed me a polystyrene cup of coffee from the terminal kiosk and I sat in the boat savouring the moment.

This was Sunday. Term started again on Monday so we needed to get on the ferry which was already approaching the linkspan. The weather in the sound was not causing Lord of The Isles as much trouble as it had caused us but, even so, it was the first sailing since Friday because of the gale. The boat was fully booked. There was not even deck space for the kayaks.

The vehicle queue was full of cars and lorries, with drivers equally desperate to be away. We identified a large bodied van and tapped on the window to awaken the driver. In the best traditions of travellers in wild places offering help to one another we arranged for 12 kayaks – our own and those from the Jura expedition I had seen earlier – to be loaded into the empty Mother's Pride lorry and taken on the ferry.

There was just time for the four of us to order full Scottish breakfasts in the nearby cafe. 'Are you the guys who've been living off seaweed in a cave for a week?' asked the waitress. We said that was a slight exaggeration but basically true. 'Yer breakfasts are on the house then.' She said. It turned out she had done a bit of paddling in her time and had been impressed'.

'Have you got any more trips planned, Nigel?' Caroline asked.

'No, I've got two steel hips, and hardly anything else works as it once did,' he said. 'The body takes quite a lot of punishment over the years doing what *we did every summer, I don't think I did myself any good, physically*'.

'Nigel, if you'd known when you started, what you know now, would you do anything differently?' I asked.

'Yes, I'd start younger and do more – a lot more.' He said. 'We were four blokes, in the prime of life and at the top of our game, doing things most others couldn't do. It was a form of elitism I suppose. We were together but each of us taking the challenge separately. We paddled long hours, sought out empty beaches, on uninhabited islands, in some of the most beautiful places on Earth. We kept our own councils a lot of the time.

You learn a lot about your inner self when you have only a small stove and a driftwood fire to keep warm and prepare food that you have carried with you or caught. After the clamour of a grasping, striving career you learn there are very few things you actually need in order to be content – food, shelter and warmth; somewhere not too lumpy to sleep, perhaps a book to read and companions that don't ask too much of you. We were so stripped down that even the dolphins recognised us. People watching from cliff tops as we passed would marvel at us, and the dolphins. We had the same, special kind of freedom.'

Nigel Laybourne and kayak.

CHAPTER 6

The Gaelic Language – As it was and as it is today

GAELIC IS A European language, just like any other European language. Whether you decide to call it a modern language depends on your point of view and, to a certain extent, your politics. Carol MacNeill, recently retired primary headteacher on the tiny Scottish island of Colonsay, showed me a folder of student resources for the teaching of Gaelic which was instantly recognisable as a folder of classroom material for language teaching, just as I might find in a French, German or Spanish classroom anywhere. There were the flashcards, dominoes and the labelled scenes with which language teachers are familiar.

The issues for Gaelic teaching are different from those surrounding French, German or Spanish, however. Gaelic is certainly a minority language, spoken by people often geographically isolated from large population centres by seas and mountains. The electronic communication revolution is being put to very good use by relatively small numbers of people in remote locations, to compensate them for the difficulties of travelling to centres for their Gaelic instruction. One group of students in Scotland is learning Gaelic, online, with the help of a tutor recently moved to live in Spain.

To fully understand the social, political and educational reasons behind the current drive to strengthen Gaelic speaking in Scotland it is necessary to know something of the language's history – a history which is the history of Scotland itself.

Gaelic is one of a family of Celtic languages which formerly prevailed in Alba (Scotland), Eire, Man, Wales, Cornwall, Brittany, Spain, Portugal, France, Holland and further east. Today they are confined largely to just Scotland, Eire, Man, Cornwall and Brittany.

Gaels originally came to Scotland from Ireland. They settled in present day Argyll which they called Dal Riata. In 843 the Picts and Gaels were united by a Gaelic leader – Kenneth MacAlpin – and the country of Alba (most of present day Scotland north of the

Forth and Clyde rivers) was formed. MacAlpin is often referred to as the first King of Scotland.

The Vikings had their say around the first millennium but were eventually driven out by Somerled who established the Lordship of the Isles and the beginning of the clan system. The Lordship was a flourishing Gaelic culture, based in the west, until it was broken by James III in 1493. Following the union of the crowns under James VI of Scotland (James I of England) in 1603 the Jacobites needed the Gaelic clan chiefs to help rule Scotland.

The union of the Scottish and English Parliaments came in 1707 but the Jacobites rose again several times, most famously in 1745 when Charles Edward Stuart (Bonnie Prince Charlie) attempted to reclaim the throne for his father. Bonnie Prince Charlie's rebellion was crushed at Culloden in 1746 and after that the British Government set about eradicating Gaelic culture. The wearing of tartan and the playing of bagpipes were outlawed and land was taken, leading eventually to Gaels being ruthlessly cleared from the straths and glens to make way for the massive sheep estates of landlords during the 19th century. Many emigrated, some forcibly, especially to Canada.

In the late 19th century Gaels started to fight back, particularly in the Gaelic strongholds of Skye and Lewis. In 1886 crofters were given security of tenure in the Crofters' Act but Gaelic was still discouraged. By 1970 it was dying. Many Gaels today can still remember being punished for speaking it at school. Mairi McKay (84), who has lived her entire life in the Hebrides, remembers being taught that it was rude to continue speaking the Gaelic if an English speaker entered the room.

The revival started in 1975 with the formation of *Comhairle nan Eilean Siar* (The Western Isles Council) which was the first statutory, public body to recognise and use Gaelic as part of their day to day work. It introduced bi-lingual education in some schools.

In 1982 Gaelic playgroups were formed and in 1984 *Comunn na Gàidhlig* (CNAG) was set up with a remit to support, promote and develop Gaelic throughout Scotland. There are now Gaelic units in primary schools, a Gaelic Secondary school in Glasgow, Gaelic Youth Clubs and Gaelic TV and radio programmes.

A new Gaelic economy is emerging. At *Sabhal Mòr Òstaig* on Skye and Lews Castle College in Stornoway, Isle of Lewis, full time vocational courses are taught through the medium of Gaelic. There are *Fèisean* (traditional Gaelic festivals) and *mods* (Gaelic music and arts competitions). In 1999 the Scottish Parliament appointed a Minister for Gaelic and a Gaelic Officer to allow use of the language in parliamentary debates.

A number of school children in Scotland are in Gaelic medium education (receiving education in subjects other than languages through the medium of Gaelic). In addition secondary school students are able to study Gaelic as an option subject. In 2006 the Glasgow Gaelic School opened with around 200 students up to the age of 18 receiving their entire education in Gaelic.

One of the major problems facing the wider provision of Gaelic teaching is the shortage of qualified teachers. Distance learning courses are being run and, in some cases, teachers need to further develop their IT skills before they can access the courses. Tobermory High School on the Isle of Mull, for example, is working with *Stòrlann*, based in Kershader, Isle of Lewis, on the development of a distance learning, Gaelic medium geography course. Many teachers have first boosted their computer skills through The Learning Schools Programme. Aberdeen University also offers a distance learning course for Gaelic medium teachers.

Teachers throughout Scotland typically meet in small groups via video-conferencing to develop their own Gaelic skills prior to teaching it in their schools. Electronic links are especially useful for teachers on islands. The new GLOW system allows teachers and pupils throughout Scotland to interact through the internet. It is the next generation of video conferencing – available to all. Such meetings are no substitute for face to face encounters but, nevertheless, when the alternative is a two and a half hour boat journey and an overnight stay on the mainland these type of courses are invaluable.

There are also masterclass training sessions, especially designed for Gaelic teachers. These sessions are taking place in Stirling, Inverness and the Western Isles. The Glasgow Gaelic School will also act as a hub to support national provision and develop the Gaelic medium secondary provision and especially the virtual secondary network. The BBC is also involved and the very significant resource base in their digital curriculum will be harnessed.

The Gaelic Medium Teachers' Action Group, established in 2005 has pledged to work for more part time and distance learning courses and better career prospects for Gaelic medium teachers. A range of online e-learning materials is being commissioned and links are being made *Am Baile,* the bilingual, digital archive of Scottish history and culture. *Gàidhlig Air-loidhne* is a website, in Gaelic only, for Gaelic teachers. The team visits schools, provides games, worksheets, forums and competitions to promote Gaelic learning. An online drama course using *fèin-mheas* (self-assessment) is now available.

Gaelic speaking Gillebride MacMillan, originally from South Uist, has been working with pupils at five schools as part of the *Cruinn-eòlas aig Astar* pilot project. It allows s1 and s2 pupils to study geography through Gaelic online tutorials and classroom mentors. The schools involved in the £70,000 Executive funded project are: Greenfaulds Academy, Cumbernauld, Islay High School, Plockton High School, Tain Royal Academy, Forfar Academy, Ardnamurchan High School and Tobermory. Pupils receive online support from Mr MacMillan, who marks their work and monitors progress from his home in Spain.

Classroom mentors are also on hand to provide support in each school. Similar courses – in history, modern studies and maths – are currently being planned by the Gaelic ICT Implementation group. Mr MacMillan said 'There is a big change for pupils who have gone through Gaelic medium primary education. They go from hearing Gaelic all day to, perhaps, only two hours a week in secondary school.'

The older folk in Gaelic speaking communities have been invaluable to the schools in providing a reservoir of speakers, to go into schools and speak with the children, perhaps over lunch in an informal way. Gaelic as a living, spoken language has been to the edge of oblivion and looked over. It was getting to the point that only a few Gaelic poets and songwriters were keeping it going. Bands such as Capercaille and Runrig have carried the torch these past thirty years with lines such as: 'Only the bards are preserving our identity.' (Runrig) There is certainly more to the Scottish identity than the language of Gaelic, but Gaelic was the language of the peat-cutters, crofters, fisherman and fowlers. It is the tongue of the highlanders and islanders and it is a most appropriately poetic language with which to describe the most beautiful country. It is an ancient language, with no words for computer, internet or digital revolution, but these instruments may yet be its salvation.

CHAPTER 7

Colonsay – Hidden treasure island

COLONSAY HIDES HER CHARMS from the world very well. There are few casual visitors to Colonsay, you have to make the two-hour passage from Oban deliberately and then, as you sail along the island's eastern shore, searching for the tiny harbour at Scalasaig, you wonder why you bothered. Even the Vikings and Lords of the Isles had to make quite an effort to get here as Colonsay isn't on the way to anywhere in particular. Plunging waterfalls, mountains and picturesque lighthouses are conspicuous by their absence.

The approaching ferry passes close by the deserted fishing village of *Riasg Buidhe* then, a little further along, the newer houses at Glassard, to which the fisher folk moved during the 1920s. For much of the year the first sign of colour is Keith Rutherford's red post van, parked outside the post office, and the whitewashed hotel standing half a mile or so back from the pier.

At last you know you are here and soon the social gathering at the pier head, that meets every ferry, turns a human face to your arrival. You have crossed the sea and are safe in this tiny haven. Incredibly, it seems, there's a telephone box, a shop, a dog on a lead and a child on a bike. There's May McKinnon's Pantry, sheep, houses and a little road leading inland that you can hardly wait to explore. The Lords of the Isles were not disappointed either. They found a strategic stronghold from which to watch over the sea-lanes from Mull and Iona to the north; Jura, Islay, Kintyre and Ireland in the south.

Accommodation is plentiful and varied, but not limitless, so you'll need to book in advance. The hotel, *The Colonsay*, is the social centre of the island with nine comfortable bedrooms, a tastefully modern restaurant, bar meals and a pub quiz on Thursdays. *The Colonsay* has been refurbished in recent years with laird, Alex Howard, as one of the directors. '*The Colonsay* is for everyone,' he said when I met him recently. 'If you want to sit by the fire, on the steps outside or in the bar you can. If you want to kick off your wellies and find somewhere quiet to read a book you can. If you want to eat good, un-pretentious food, and have it served by attentive staff, who will talk you through the wine list in the restaurant, well you can do that too.' It is all true.

The estate also offers about 20 holiday cottages sleeping between four and 12 people and there are holiday flats in The Big House – Colonsay House, surrounded by the policy woodland and the home farm up at Kiloran. There is even a backpacker's hostel in the old game keeper's lodge. You will need to contact the Cottage Office – they will take your booking, light the fire for your arrival, organise coal supplies, pick you up from the ferry and chase down the pier after you at the end of your stay with your camera, binoculars or anything else you left behind.

The road from the pier in the east reaches the sea again in the west at the golf course. After the grey sea and the low, grey-brown rocks of the approach to Colonsay the gentle, green pasture of the hinterland is both a delight and a surprise.

The island is almost cut in two by the three pools of Loch Fada and the single track road here runs by fields of grazing sheep and cattle (although most of the sheep do appear to be on the road). My favourite cottage – Longfield – is just by the roadside and the sunsets behind Dhu Artach lighthouse in the cold, clear spring air can be – well, cold, clear and sunny. Utterly peaceful – peaceful that is if you don't mind the corncrakes rasping away at dusk, the snipe drumming or the oystercatchers calling from down in the bay at Port Mhor. Even the cattle grid has been replaced recently, so you don't hear it rattle anymore.

The bookshop used to be here at Port Mhor. Kevin Byrne (Harbourmaster, school bus driver, former hotelier, writer and island publisher) converted a derelict generator shed into *The Colonsay Bookshop and House of Lochar Publishers,* selling and publishing books with a Scottish and local feel from a floor space which, although tiny, was probably in proportion to Foyle's of London when one considers the size and population of Colonsay. In 2012 Kevin moved to larger premises at Scalasaig and the old generator shed now houses a small display for the heritage trust.

Further along the road the settlement of Kilchatten includes the school (six children), the Baptist church and the cemetery. It would comfort me to know I was to spend eternity in a spot as glorious as this, pushing up such a profusion of daisies, not to mention flag irises, marsh marigolds and a myriad of other flowers each spring. The straggle of Kilchatten houses backs onto the hillside which both protects them from the Atlantic gales and affords them elevated views over the loch.

Past the old mill in a wooded valley, now a holiday cottage but still complete with wheel and stream, there is Kiloran farm and Colonsay House, elements of which survive from the original 1722 dwelling. The gardens can be visited on payment of £2 on certain afternoons in the summer and tea can be taken on the terraced lawn.

For no money at all you can wander round the rhododendron woods at any time and you might bump into Jean McAllister pushing (or dragging) her battered pram through the woods, laden with rhododendron logs for the fire. 'I go for my roddies every day,' she told me. 'Alex lets me take the wee ones. The tracks play havoc with my wheels though,' she said. 'The trouble is there's a real shortage of old prams on Colonsay, you couldn't bring me one the next time you come could you?'

In the woods, Jean does a passable impersonation of an old charcoal burner but actually her only experience with the stuff was as a drawing medium at Glasgow School of Art. Jean's house by Kiloran farm is her studio where she produces much sought after and very accomplished collages of life on Colonsay. The one that hangs in my room was a commission for a special birthday – it shows the ancient fortress of Dun Gallain from across the bay at Machrins. 'The wee boat with the red sail that I've put in your picture was diddling backwards and forwards across the bay one day when I was down there with the grandchildren,' Jean said.

Beyond the house one of the most perfect beaches in the world is just a ten minute walk away at Kiloran Bay. A half mile wide sweep of clean sand, backed by steep dunes and *machair* grazing for the cattle of nearby Balnahard farm. The Queen often came ashore here for a picnic on her annual cruise in *Britannia* but, less certain is the claim that Bonnie Prince Charlie landed on Colonsay in 1745 to ask the laird for help. The prince was listened to politely but the request was denied out of allegiance to the British Crown – so I expect Her Majesty feels quite safe on the beach these days.

Kiloran Bay is at the end of the tarmac road but you can walk over Colonsay's mountain range, with *Carnan Eoin* the highest at 469 feet, and on to Balnahard beach in the north east corner of the island. You might see golden eagles, choughs and will certainly be able to scoop up handfuls of tiny cowrie shells from a special corner of yet another stunning beach.

My favourite walk is across the Strand at the south end of Colonsay. For a couple of hours either side of low water you can walk across to Oronsay where there is a farm house and a 14th century Augustinian priory dedicated to St Columba. It is said that the holy man landed here in AD563 but could still see Ireland so carried on to Iona where he first established Christianity in Britain. Nevertheless the Oronsay priory probably matched the Iona church in size and importance in its heyday.

St Columba is credited with establishing the Christian Church in these islands but that may not have been his plan when he left Ireland. He was, it is said, fleeing political pressure back home so it is a re-assuring thought that when we come to Colonsay to get away from the rat race, when I sit in the sun with my back to the priory wall, admire the view across to the Paps of Jura and listen to the gulls, I am maintaining a long tradition of escapism.

On the way across the Strand I almost always see Andrew Abrahams, the oyster farmer, driving his tractor between the beds and his isolated house on the hillside. As the tide falls I hurry across at the earliest opportunity so there is still a paddle in the icy water needed to reach Oronsay. I always enjoy this part of the walk but I have seen a few southern softies dangling their legs off the back of Andrew's trailer on the trip.

Andrew can only 'work the tides' for about half of each month so he tends his bees while the oysters are having their meals, and produces Colonsay's wildflower honey for sale to visitors in the shop and the Pantry. The Strand is an atmospheric, wild, wide open space. When the sun shines in the spring it is easy to see shell-fish farming as an idyllic, stress-free commune with nature, certainly the commute by tractor across the beach beats the M25, but Andrew wears full oilskins, even on a sunny day. The weather can change here very quickly and the Atlantic gales tears through the gap between Colonsay and Oronsay for days on end in the winter.

The Strand is clearly visible from the final approach of the eight-seater Islander aircraft that provides the twice daily service from Connel, on the mainland, to Colonsay's new airfield. The locals are divided over the new development. There are those who say:

'It's no good to me. I can't afford £80 for the single fare and, anyway, when I come back from Oban I like to bring a month's supply of shopping and there isn't room for that.'

Alex Howard believes that, like so many developments, people will take advantage of it and it will be good for business initiatives on the island. I put the ecological objections to him but his quick and ready response was: 'What is worse, a 2,000 ton ferry carrying six people, and burning all that diesel, or a light aircraft arriving?' On the other ecological issue exercising minds at present – wind power – he was equally forthright: 'We already have mains electricity and, besides, the cable from Islay cannot carry electricity *away* from Colonsay so we couldn't use it to export power,' he said. 'Wind power does not make economic sense if the tax breaks are taken away.' The Laird did suggest, however, that if a sound and sensible proposal was put forward he might go along with it eventually. 'Provided there is a watertight exit clause to the agreement – ready for when wind power goes out of fashion.'

Alex Howard is certainly no destructive exploiter of the environment for profit, he has grown up with a true sense of guardianship. His own children went to the primary school here and he is sensitive to the need to manage the estate for the benefit of locals, visitors and the wildlife, whilst hopefully turning a profit at the same time. He sees these interests as inter-connected anyway. He is fiercely proud of the tree regeneration taking place on the hillside behind Scalasaig. 'The whole stretch up from the village to Turramen Loch is covered with rowan and birch we've planted – it will soon be a mature, native woodland.'

Colonsay has an ageing population and very few full-time employment opportunities. The drain of youngsters to the mainland for education and work is a common island problem and Colonsay is no exception.

A Norwegian company has offered to stimulate the island economy with the installation of salmon cages. According to the Colonsay online newsletter, Marine Harvest offered £50,000 up front and £10,000 a year to the community if there is a majority in favour of the fish farm. There would be six, full-time jobs for which locals would be given every consideration. It is a tempting offer but has split island opinion and '...*caused a lot of fall-outs*' said one local.

'We need jobs. It would be wrong of us old folk to oppose the farm and deny opportunities to the youngsters someone told me. 'So long as they don't poison the sea we should go for it.'

Marine Harvest promises minimal pollution. Waste from the fish is dispersed by strong currents and there is no impact beyond the footprint of the cages. Pesticides, used to kill fish lice, are not detectable beyond 200m, according to recent research.

Protestors point to visual impact from the 12 cages sited 1,500 yards off-shore on the east side of the island. They would be seen from some homes (two miles away) and by visitors to *Riasg Buidhe*. The arriving and departing ferry from Oban would also pass close by.

Fish cages don't seem too bad to me. I remember seeing my first, on Mull, 30 years ago and thinking it unremarkable. I would want assurances about environmental impact, of course, but people have to work – and eat. One islander told me: 'Marine Harvest seems quite reasonable, if we don't say yes to them then someone else will come and do it anyway.'

In the end we cannot expect islands to be museums or picture post cards, just so we can go to look at them, not unless we go in larger numbers and that would bring its own problems.

A friend once said to me: 'I don't understand your fascination with the wilds of Scotland – I like to see human influence in the environment.' I know what he meant. I am glad that people live and work and thrive here. *Runrig* sang about *'empty glens'* but they were not singing their praises.

In 2013 the islanders voted for the fish farm. A turn-out of 91 per cent cast 67 votes for and 43 against allowing Norwegian company, Marine Harvest, to install salmon cages in the sea off Colonsay. Operations should begin in 2015.

Artist's garden, Colonsay.

CHAPTER 8

Oransay – Sanctuary island

YOU CAN QUIBBLE THAT Oransay is not an island if you wish but, for me, it is one of the most beautifully peaceful islands in Scotland. Oransay is attached to Colonsay by a wide expanse of shell sand called the Strand which is exposed for a maximum of about five hours at low tide, allowing a safe walk across. Colonsay is first reached by a two hour ferry ride from Oban and then, after checking the state of the tide with Keith Rutherford at the post office, you may have time for coffee in *the Pantry* or the *Colonsay Hotel* before crossing to Oransay.

The Strand can be a bleak, windswept place in winter but on a good day it makes a lovely walk. The ebbing tide leaves a shallow channel at the Oransay shore necessitating a brief, cold paddle before stepping on to dry land again – but it adds to the fun. The Oransay track leaves the beach and moves inland through a pass in the rocks, round the base of Beinn Oransay and across to the farmland on the southern shore. Apart from the post van, farm tractor and RSPB land rover there is no traffic on Oransay and the quiet view from the high point of the road, across the *machair* and the glittering sea to the Paps of Jura and Islay, is one of the finest in the Hebrides.

Human hunter-gatherers came to Oransay during the Mesolithic period some 8,000 years ago. Their shell mound middens that have been excavated here are some of the oldest traces of human habitation in Scotland. They built wood and skin shelters and exploited fish and shellfish from the shore for food. They had fire and roasted hazelnuts. They left behind them fragments of flint tools for us to speculate over.

Close by the beach and the middens is the substantial ruin of a beautiful 14th century Augustinian priory – possibly on the site of St Oran's original sixth century monastery. The cloisters, celtic cross and several sculpted medieval tombstones make the priory an interesting visit.

The farm on Oransay is owned by Mrs Frances Colburn and

managed by RSPB Scotland, principally for the benefit of two endangered bird species – the red-billed chough and the corncrake. The corncrake, a quail-like bird, was once widespread in Britain but its decline can be traced back to the advent of horse powered, mechanised haymaking. The birds like to feed, move around and nest on the ground in tall vegetation (hayfields) and found it difficult to escape the blades as reapers moved faster and faster.

The adult corncrakes arrive from Africa in April and May – usually returning to where they hatched or bred the previous year – and the males begin their distinctive calling – often from dusk to dawn. The sound has been likened to someone running their fingers across the teeth of a comb. *Crex crex* (the bird's Latin name) is a good, onomatopoeic name for the corncrake. In March, Mike Peacock the RSPB man on Oransay, closes several of the in-bye fields and puts the cattle and sheep out on the hill grazing. The hay and silage crops are then not cut until the first week of September, allowing the corncrakes to use them as cover to raise two broods. Two broods are essential for the population to increase and RSPB has designated Oransay a corncrake recovery area. Even then the cutting is done slowly, starting in the middle and working outwards to allow the flightless chicks and moulting adults to run for cover elsewhere. 'Corncrake corners' and 'Corncrake corridors' are also provided – patches and strips of nettles and irises into which the birds can hide while they wait for the hay to grow and after it is cut. Mike's front 'lawn', just under his bedroom window, is one such sanctuary and he has become used to sleeping through their chorus.

The red-billed chough is a member of the crow family with glossy black plumage, a striking red bill and red legs. Its broad wings are deeply 'fingered' giving it aerial mastery like a bird of prey. It is found in only a handful of British sites outside of Oransay and Colonsay. Choughs feed on the ground, digging insects and their grubs from loose soil, sand and especially cow pats. The management of Oronsay, putting the cattle and sheep on the hill in summer, provides the necessary short grass and dung to support the choughs. They need a very contrasting habitat to the corncrake. The sandy, well-drained soil in the *machair* (see below) and dunes is often rich in invertebrate food for choughs such as mining bees and dung insects. In the autumn and winter there is also good feeding on kelp-fly maggots from rotting seaweed on the beach.

Choughs, like corncrakes, were once widespread in Britain but, since the 19th century, have become lost from England and (almost) from mainland Scotland. The loss of mixed, low-intensity farming and grazing has contributed to the decline. Some anti-parasitic cattle treatments can affect the variety of invertebrates in dung so Mike is selective and sparing in their use. Oransay choughs have also been affected by the gapeworm – a parasitic worm that lives in their windpipes leaving them seriously debilitated. The population had peaked at 25 pairs but fell back to around 14 or 15 because of the worm.

Sand and shell particles from the west facing beaches on Oransay have, for thousands of years, been blown inland to form low-lying, shell-sand dunes and plains. This *machair* (pronounced makker) is one of the rarest and most fragile habitats in Europe. Half of all *machair* is in the Outer Hebrides but some of the finest is on Oransay. The *machair* sand contains 80–90 per cent shell fragments and this distinguishes it from the 'links' of eastern Scotland. *Machair* hosts a kaleidoscopic array of plant species – from daisy and buttercup to a list of perhaps 500, it is a botanist's paradise. The Outer Hebrides, Coll, Tiree, Iona and others each have characteristic flower communities on their *machairs* and the one on Oransay is home to adder's tongue fern, moonwort, marsh orchid and thyme, plus the rare marsh fritillary butterfly, belted beauty moth and mining bee. *Machair* is not a pristine, wild habitat as it depends on agricultural grazing to prevent it turning into rank grassland and this is part of the management of Oransay. Apart from the cattle and sheep the *machair* is home to farmland birds such as skylark, twite and linnet. There are breeding lapwing, oystercatcher, dunlin, ringed plover, redshank and snipe. In the winter the whooper swans and barnacle geese arrive from the north for their own kind of sanctuary. There is a nationally important colony of grey seals, as well as common seals sharing the rocks and skerries with arctic terns. There are great northern divers in the bays.

No serious predators live on Oransay, apart from the odd peregrine, but *machair* communities can be devastated by animals such as rats and mink. Four hedgehogs were released on South Uist in 1974 and have produced a population of around 5,000 with dire consequences for the ground nesting waders. Attempts at their control have been only partially successful.

As you walk across the Strand to Oransay, usually on a calm, sunny day because you will have waited for such an opportunity, everything seems to slow down. You may see Keith the Post in his red land rover or Andrew Abrahams driving his tractor, at walking pace, through the last of the ebb. Andrew will be heading to his oyster beds in the Oransay intertidal zone. The oysters are immersed twice a day by the cold, clean, food rich water of the North Atlantic. Like the *machair* this is a fragile place. One oil spill could ruin it.

Andrew's other job is bee keeping, and he believes St Columba would have brought bees from Ireland as a necessary part of establishing his new community – the honey will have been used medicinally and the wax helpful for the long winter nights. It is satisfying to know that the simple, natural food chain of sunlight, to honey, for people endures in this peaceful place. I cannot think of anywhere else in Britain where the people are more in tune with the land and sea, and guarding them with such love.

Legend has it that fugitives from justice could receive absolution if they were able to cross the Strand. They would then have to spend a year and a day at the priory. The hunter-gatherers came here and found a home. Corncrakes fly from Africa each year and their tiny, Hebridean population clings at the edge of local extinction thanks to the efforts of a few people who prepare the way for them by guarding the nettles and irises. St Columba considered Oransay for his sanctuary, I just hope he didn't disturb the nesting choughs when he walked up the hill. King George VI said: 'We do not own the land, we hold it on trust for those who will come after us.' I think he would be very pleased with the job being done on Oransay.

CHAPTER 9

Lunga – Not your average school nature ramble

WE SAILED TO LUNGA in an open boat, pitching and rolling across six miles of Atlantic swell west of Mull. Twenty, advanced level biology students, and their teachers, travelling to study the seabirds – not your average nature ramble.

Lunga is one of the Treshnish Isles, a group including Dutchman's Cap, Fladda and the Cairn na Burghs (Cairn na Burgh More and Cairn na Burgh Beg). This tiny cluster lies six miles north of Iona from whence we sailed, passing Staffa halfway across. This is Lord of the Isles territory and a defensive castle, the remains of which can still be seen on Cairn na Burgh More is thought to have belonged to the Lord Of Lorn, Chief of the Clan MacDougall some 650 years ago.

There was only one, narrow path up to the ramparts and it is said this was defended at night by the sentry rolling boulders down at intervals to skittle over anyone creeping up. The day shift would carry the boulders back again, ready for the next night.

Lunga is the largest of the group. We landed near Castle Rock in the north-west and set up camp on the grassy cliff-top plateau by the ruined village. There were grand views to the north, west and east. Behind the camp was the 337 ft summit of Cruachan, the highest point of this volcanic island.

We met with some bird ringers from the British Trust for Ornithology (BTO), there to record breeding seabirds for which Lunga is an important haven. Since our visit, the island has been designated a Site of Special Scientific Interest – it provides breeding sites for guillemot, razorbill, puffin, shag, fulmar and kittiwake, together with manx shearwater and storm petrel. The auks are concentrated on harp rock, a precipitous stack separated from the main island by a narrow chasm through which the sea surges 100 feet below.

The BTO chaps were, understandably, not too impressed when

we appeared at the top of the cliff. I have thought about this many times since and I now believe that, had the roles been reversed, I may well have thrown myself off the opposite cliff. I have imagined spending all winter anticipating my quiet week on Lunga only to see a class of school children pitching camp 100 yards away. It is the stuff of nightmares.

I am not known for my diplomacy but I think the first five minutes after we met the ringers must count as my finest hour. We explained that we did have permission to be there, that we had come, like them, for serious bird study and that we would keep out of their way. As tension ebbed away they let slip that they were running out of milk and toilet paper. Half an hour later I picked two of our most personable students and sent them over with generous supplies of the needed items. It had the desired effect and must have been much like the gifts of beads and mirrors made by earlier explorers. Thereafter the bird ringers made us very welcome and showed our students things we never could. They must have been born teachers and experienced something of the thrill to be had when someone shows an interest in one's passions.

In earlier times, in many parts of the Hebrides, seabird eggs provided important seasonal food. On Lunga, bird-hunters would crawl over to Harp Rock on a boat's mast carried up for the purpose and laid across the gap. At least one poor soul fell to his death in the attempt. On St Kilda, 80 odd miles to the west, men were world famous for their fowling skills. They were brought up to a life of climbing the crags to collect, not just the eggs, but also young and adult birds for meat, oil and feathers. A St Kildan's most prized possession was his horse-hair rope with which his colleagues would lower him to the most difficult ledges. It was said the St Kildan's feet and toes aided them on the bird-cliffs, having adapted to their life by becoming elongated and almost prehensile. St Kildan's were consummate cragsmen but, for all that, there were many who did not die in their beds.

The birds of Harp Rock were obliging in their preference for particular flight paths as they approached their nests. They would fly in at cliff edge level, along the gap between rock and island, then bank steeply before performing a controlled stall and touching down. This made the task of catching them for ringing a simple one, requiring only an over-sized butterfly net and a good eye. The ringers could stand at the edge and select the birds they wanted as they flew in line astern at the chasm. It was like watching planes approaching Heathrow.

We stood back as ringers brought puffins, razorbills and guillemots for us in the hand. When, for so long, you have seen these birds through binoculars, it is startling to hold them. I was stunned by the detail in every feather – one slightly out of place here, one a slightly odd colour there. Birds are warm-blooded creatures but, even so, it was a surprise, and a joy, to feel the body heat coming from deep within them. Somehow you expect something that was bobbing about on a cold sea a few moments earlier to be, well, cold. The students were also struck by how small and delicate the birds were – another shock in an animal leading such a tough life – but, in fact, the life expectancy of the birds is quite long. If they make it past the first year they can expect to live 30 or even 40 years. This is even more remarkable when you consider that, with the exception of a few summer weeks at the breeding cliffs, they live entirely at sea, although it is the weeks on the ledges or in the burrows that are the most hazardous, with predation by rats or gulls a constant threat.

Our students had been studying a genetic trait in guillemots that results in some birds having a distinctive white stripe down each side of the face – the so-called 'bridled' form. The frequency of bridled birds increases the further north you go, and guillemots are distributed way up beyond the Arctic Circle. One student was holding a guillemot and happened to comment on this to the BTO man. 'Hang on a wee minute,' he said 'I'll get you a bridled one.' He went down to the edge with his net and was back two minutes later, gently holding a guillemot with a beautiful white stripe on either side of its head.

Lunga is a mile long a few hundred yards wide. There is a path, of sorts, all the way round, and the trip can be made at a leisurely pace in an afternoon. The walk takes you past grey seals sunning themselves on the rocks, and clumps of pink thrift – my favourite of all the Hebridean flowers. Lunga is an island of two halves. Cruachan fills the northern half, with the path running round its base to the old village served by at least two clear wells – still lined and capped by flat stones. In the south, the island drops to a lower level and is almost cut in half at a narrow waist. For adventurous school students there is a subterranean access to the beach on the west side.

It's amazing how hungry you get in the fresh air of the islands, and how far you walk without realising it when, at every step, you are assailed by some new sound or sight. After studying the seabirds we strolled round the south end and took the path back to the village round the base of Cruachan. Nesting shags gronked at us from among huge fallen boulders. We scrambled back up to Camp Plateau and got the Trangia stoves going under pans full of rice and tins of assorted stews.

One glorious sunset, several Beatles' songs and a warming camp-fire later we were back to work on the shingle beach between the base of the cliff and Castle Rock. The BTO had set up mist nets to catch night-flying storm petrels for ringing. Mist nets are like delicate badminton nets, suspended between bamboo poles stuck in the ground and into which petrels fly – to be ringed, weighed and released unharmed.

The storm petrels are tiny by seabird standards so they only return to their nest holes after dark – to avoid the predatory gulls and skuas. Soon there were so many birds being caught that one of the nets was taken down to allow the ringers to process all the arrivals in reasonable time.

With the petrels safely ringed and released, and the time ticking past 1am, it was announced the next job was to walk along the grassy flanks of Cruchan to listen for shearwaters coming home. Manx shearwaters are vulnerable in the same way as petrels and so they, too, only land at night – in the darkest part of the night at that.

The returning bird will circle off-shore, calling to its mate in the burrow to announce it is ready to take over egg- or chick-sitting duty. The call has been described as like a screaming baby. The time to start shining your torch on the grass is when the wailing stops: that's when you know the incoming bird is about to land. A shearwater's legs are set well back under its body, which makes it very agile on water and in the air, but hopeless on land. It more or less crashes into the grass and then scrambles into its burrow as quickly as possible to avoid becoming a late supper for some big gull.

I taught biology for almost 30 years and met students whom I will remember for all manner of reasons and one such is Robert. Robert, aka Mr Cool, was 17 years old. I thought he had only come on the trip for the time off school and the company of the girls. Nothing had appeared to impress him thus far. It was getting cold on the hillside, the shearwater arrivals had slowed down and we hadn't caught more than a fleeting glimpse of one. Robert had walked off a few paces from us when, out of the darkness, his voice carried towards us in the most joyous, excited, child-like innocence I have ever heard from a big lad. He was struggling to convey urgency, yet whisper at the same time. All efforts at being cool had gone. He just wanted us to see what he was seeing. 'Sir, there's one here, still outside its burrow.' The BTO man walked over and carefully picked up the shearwater. 'You hold it, sir,' someone said quietly. I could feel its heart beating and its incredible warmth. I could see the shine in Robert's eyes. It was two o'clock in the morning and this was the best teaching I had ever done. It still is.

During this visit we took nothing but photographs and left nothing but footprints. Turf was lifted for the campfire and replaced afterwards. We sought to keep the environmental impact of our visit to the absolute minimum. I believe the environmental aware-ness raised in the youngsters justified our presence.

I should like to place on record my deep appreciation of the generosity shown by the four BTO men of the Treshnish Auk Ringing Group.

Robert, by the way, is a captain in the Royal Marines now. I see him occasionally and he has never forgotten that night on the hill-side in Lunga. I know I never will.

CHAPTER 10

Lunga – As close as you can get to nature

THERE ARE FEW moments more evocative of adventure than a sleeper train departure. Make the train bound for a border crossing, heading for the ocean and you have a real thrill. The only drawback of the Euston to Oban service is the early morning change in Glasgow, but the mountain train to the sea more than compensates. Ninety miles in three hours gives plenty of opportunity to view the mountains, lochs and waterfalls as we chug – it is a diesel locomotive these days, but I still like to think we chug – uphill, into the Argyll heartland.

My favourite bit is the 10 minute stop at Crianlarich where the train divides – for Oban and Mallaig – and there is time for tea and a bun at the station cafe. The stretch of legs, the mountain air and the temporary pause, as well as the bun, are nostalgic of a time when travel was a thrill and arriving less certain. I walk to the end of the platform, turning my back on fellow travellers and dwell on the feeling of the Highlands. There is a frisson to the journey.

At Tyndrum the Oban train bears left on the single track running along the floor of Glen Lochy. It is no accident the engineers chose this route. After the Ice Age the River Lochy was forced this way, then the Highland cattle drovers and road builders chose it as the simplest way up from the sea. For mile after mile the river meanders whilst road and rail are squeezed between it and the hill side. This narrow pass is less than 1,000 feet above sea level but it is mountain country. The train sidles by Loch Awe and Kilchurn Castle – built by Campbells, besieged by MacGregors and relieved by Cromwell. Scotland's history is punctuated by these fractious episodes, repeated at a thousand castles throughout the land.

We crossed from Oban, via Mull and Iona, to be voluntarily marooned on the deserted Treshnish island of Lunga – about a mile long by a half wide, with the roofless, stone skeletons of a few old houses looking out across a raised, grassy plateau. The stones were glowing golden where they faced the horizontal rays of the late sun. We camped and drew water from a good well we'd been tipped off about. Across a sound are the smaller outcrops of Cairn na Burgh, ancient fortress island of the Lords of the Isles. Even having got to Lunga I want to cross to Carn na Burgh and meet the ghosts of the warriors.

For now we content ourselves, my nine year old daughter and I, watching eider ducks camouflaged on their nests at the low cliff edge. They, too, are warmed by the last of the sun. The eider's defences against predatory gulls are cryptic coloration and absolute stillness. Catherine lay on her stomach and reached under each duck to count eggs, buried in down so soft she could feel only the heat. From beneath the fifth bird a duckling-sized, webbed appendage stretched, like a drowsy foot from a Sunday morning duvet. The young naturalist slowly pulled back her hand and the leg withdrew. Catherine turned her head and I saw, in that moment, a look of joy so breathless she couldn't speak, the memory of which I carry with me always.

It was not illegal to handle these birds at the nest – they are not on Schedule 1 of The Wildlife and Countryside Act (1981) – but was it advisable? The RSPB warden I spoke to said it was a difficult question. He couldn't actively encourage it but, at the same time, understood the formative impact such experiences can have. He had accidentally disturbed many eiders simply by stumbling on them when out walking. To reduce the risk of predation he would always draw down from the edge of the nest towards the centre – just as the ducks do when leaving – to cover the eggs from view. Unless we are to ban ourselves from ever entering the wild places then such encounters will be inevitable. We should not seek to fence off the whole of the Scottish wilderness for the private enjoyment of a few – we just have to be very careful.

Should we have handled these birds in the way that we did? Perhaps not. Would I let a granddaughter do it? Absolutely. I am a teacher, and bringing the student, at her age, to that place, on that date, was among the best teaching I have ever done. It has already helped develop one informed, sensitive, lifelong environmentalist and it would do again.

Eider duckling, Lunga.

CHAPTER 11

Staffa and Stroma –
Two, very different, deserted islands

STAFFA WAS ONE OF my first islands. I first went there in 1978 and it had long since been deserted. There is no pier or landing beach so any residents would have an almost impossible task operating a boat.

Present day visitors arrive from Iona or Mull and are landed onto a flattish, wave swept rock at one of two points on the island according to tide and weather. Actually, if there is any significant weather you don't land. Even on a calm day the Atlantic swell moves the glassy sea so the surface rises and falls beneath the boat and the would-be islander must carefully time the leap ashore.

One landing place is by Fingal's Cave. The movement of water in the cave is said to have inspired the 20 year old Mendelssohn to write his *Hebrides Overture (Fingal's Cave)* after his visit in 1829. I know it's a cliché to include this fact – every writer on Staffa does it – I apologise, dear reader, but the music really does evoke the sound and movement of the sea at Staffa. Mendelssohn was unhappy with his first attempt – *The Overture to The Solitary Island* – saying: 'it did not smell enough of seagulls and salt fish.' His altered version is the one we hear today.

Camping equipment – there is nowhere else to stay – must be carried up the cliff onto the grassy plateau 130 feet above. It is green and lush and empty up there but the real magic of Staffa is in its size. At 80 acres, Staffa does not qualify in Hamish Haswell-Smith's encyclopedia of Scottish islands – he insists on a minimum size of 100 acres so as to exclude all the tiny rocks and skerries, of which there are thousands round the Scottish coast. Even so, he gives Staffa an appendix in his book – *The Scottish Islands* – because of its unique geology namely the hexagonal basalt columns forming the Great Face and from which Fingal's Cave is hewn.

From the high point of Staffa at the southern tip, above the Great Face, looking north you can see the whole island. The land dips to a low glen almost cutting Staffa in two. Fresh water trickles from the ground here, it takes a while to collect a domestic amount but it is pure and sweet and you will need it for any prolonged stay.

Beyond the valley the ground rises again to a tiny cluster of ruined sheep fanks and a dwelling. When I pitched my tent on Staffa I was naturally drawn to this spot. There is no shelter offered by the ruins – just a few low walls and piles of stones – but the place has a homely feel about it because of them. Perhaps the spirits of the former residents were there to keep me company.

Traditionally one describes small areas in terms of football pitches or tennis courts – Staffa is about 50 football pitches – but I prefer to say it takes a couple of hours to walk round at a leisurely pace. That would allow time for watching the herring gulls tending their chicks at the little colony; gazing out to sea at the neighbouring islands, admiring the tiny flowers and odd finds on the shoreline when you are able to scramble down to it.

It is a joy on uninhabited islands, to walk where people do not regularly tread. There is purity to the nature – it is unspoiled. Animals and plants live in a way they cannot when people are regularly around and it strikes you when you are there. Their litter remains untidy. A gull colony, for instance, is a terrible mess after they have left for the season. Nature in close-up doesn't often look the way it is presented in glossy picture books.

Staffa wasn't always wilderness. In 1772 Sir Joseph Banks met a solitary herdsman: 'who sang all night and regaled us with fish and milk.' Another man, his wife and daughter, lived on Staffa and were baptised in 1782. The population in 1784 was quoted at 16. In 1798 possibly the last family to live all year round on Staffa decided to leave.

There was sporadic occupation in the summer months until the end of the 19th century but nothing since. There was no community on Staffa. There would have been no public services or council responsibility for the islanders. When the time came they just packed up a few meagre possessions and sailed away. There was no public outcry, or letters to the papers, about a vanishing way of life.

Stroma is a different island altogether, it was actively farmed and inhabited by a sizeable community until 1961 when everyone left. As the family on Staffa had found over 150 years earlier, you can't take your house with you and, if there's no market for it, you must simply leave it. The Stroma folk closed their doors, leaving a lot of bulky furniture behind, and left.

By the end of the Second World War living standards on the mainland had begun to leave those on Stroma behind. There was a population of 150 but they had no nurse. There was a harbour but a poor one. The government agreed to fund 80 per cent of a harbour upgrade and building started in 1954 but by then the population had fallen to 111.

In 1952 electric lighting had been provided for John O'Groats, on the mainland just a mile away across the fierce tidal rips of the Pentland Firth. Prospects were, literally, brighter across the water and in spite of the new harbour the writing was on the wall for Stroma.

The harbour was finished in 1956 but the shop closed that year and there were only three families left by 1957 – 16 souls in all, including the lighthouse keepers. The school had only two pupils and was closed. A year later the post office closed. The last family – the Mansons – left in 1961. Cyril Annal, who owns and farms Swona, to the north of Stroma, told me that what people forgot when they built the harbour on Stroma was that there was no comparable one on the mainland. Crossings were still at the mercy of the tides.

It is an urban myth that Stroma men made so much money working on the harbour restoration that they, cynically, took the cash and funded a move to the mainland. No one could earn that much money with just two years of labouring.

When you walk on Stroma today it is a surreal experience. From a distance it looks well populated. The solid-looking houses cluster along the road but on closer inspection the windows are broken and many of the roofs are collapsing. No traffic, cats, dogs or pedestrians move along the single track road. There are still a few carts and tractors on the island but their wheels are rotting and have sunk up to up to their axles in the earth. There are ghosts here, you can feel them, using the telephone box, the rusting machinery and the blind houses.

Jimmy Simpson now owns Stroma having spent his childhood there. He farms it for sheep but who knows what the future holds? Orkney is becoming the world capital for wave and tidally generated electricity (Stroma belongs to Caithness, not Orkney, but it's near enough). It has even been suggested Stroma might make a useful stepping stone for a tunnel connecting Orkney with the Scottish mainland.

Stroma is a beautiful place. It was a wonderful home for Katie and Ruth Ord, Helen Adams, John Manson and others. Sadly, the pace of change on Stroma couldn't match that on the mainland. If electricity and a regular ferry service had arrived a few years earlier they might have stayed. If Stroma had belonged to Orkney – a council with a more developed 'island' way of thinking – then it may have survived. Margaret Green said: 'I would go back tomorrow – if I could take my washing machine.'

Many other island communities have gone the way of Stroma, some quite recently. Noss, Scarba, Fara and Inch Kenneth in the 1960s; Pabbay, Copinsay, Scarp, Taransay (BBC Castaways), and Swona in the '70s; Isle of May in 1989 and Ailsa Craig in 1990.

Whilst I would hate to see any more island communities lost, perhaps the quiet places should be left as they are. There are parts of the UK already buried under concrete and tarmac – and the planners want more. Maybe the national gradation that exists between Piccadilly and Pabbay is a good thing.

CHAPTER 12

Tiree – 'You should come in the winter'

AN ODD THING HAPPENS when you arrive at a beach. A diver, walking from the sea bed, up the shore and onto the land crosses a line, above which only land plants and animals survive. Kelp gives way to grass and, within a few steps, people are visible going about their business. Go a little bit higher and you're flying. Tiree is just such a thin sliver of dry earth between the watery deep and the endless sky. Ben Hynish, at 462 ft, is the highest hill and there are almost no others to speak of. If our diver arrived on the island at *Traigh Bhagh*, in the south, he would face a flat plain, known as the Reef, stretching clear across to Balephetrish Bay in the north, with not so much as a contour line in between. All Tiree life is here, in this thin slice.

This 'Land Beneath the Waves' is so low-lying that, they say, you can stand on the beach in the east and watch the sun go down into the sea on the west side of the island. The Tiree people live not so much *by* the sea as *on* it. They are like the halcyon, a mythical bird thought to live in a nest floating at sea and charming the wind and waves into calm – well, perhaps not the wind, but the land was anchored firmly enough during the winter gale that blew in while I was there. There is so little high ground that it would take very little for the sea to cut the island in two, or even three parts. Earthworks across the Reef keep the water of *An Fhaodhail* from bisecting the land.

It is the lack of high ground, together with Tiree's position out in the Atlantic that determines its weather. Lying west of Mull and south of the Outer Hebrides it is exposed to winds travelling thousands of miles across the ocean, with plenty of space to build up huge waves. One old crofter, Hector Cameron, used to live on the exposed Craignish Point. Somebody asked him what it was like out on the point in a big gale: 'Ach, the only shelter we have is the little bit we are getting from Nova Scotia.'

I read another story about an old crofter, Alasdair Eachainn, struggling home from Balevullin one night during the big gale of 1953 when a corn stack went past him. 'A lot of corn stacks were knocked over that night,' he said. 'I was asking around the next day if anyone had lost a corn stack but nobody had. I reckon it came down from Barra,' he said.

The school at Cornaig closes when, but not until, the wind speed reaches 50mph – severe gale – they breed them tough here.

In January 2005 heavy rain, lightning and an extreme high tide conspired with hurricane force winds (the anemometer broke when the wind reached 124 mph) to traumatise the island. Tonnes of sea water mangled railings on the pier; roads were swept away, buildings were damaged and the coast suffered decades of erosion in a couple of hours.

On that occasion there were no casualties but people elsewhere were not so lucky. Three generations of one family were drowned on South Uist, from where warnings came again recently about the threat of inundation by the sea as a result of sinking land and rising sea-levels. Islands out here may be 20 miles apart but they are neighbours, just as much as city folk in the next street.

There are no mountains here so the rain often passes straight over to fall on Mull or the mainland, which makes Tiree the sunniest place in Britain, with a record of 16.8 hours on one July day in 1936. And, lest you think the gales blow all the time, I should point out there are only about 30 days of officially gale force winds each year. Tiree is windy, sure, but it's just a good supply of fresh air most of the time.

Snow and ice are rare. The fabled Gulf Stream keeps the island too warm, although you wouldn't think so if you went for a dip in the sea. There was a fall in 2000 when some children, and even some adults, got to make snowmen for the first time. The Gulf Stream isn't enough to warm the houses though and there has always been a need for fuel in the hearth for the long, dark winter nights in the croft.

The traditional houses have walls several feet thick. They are built low and squat, with small windows and massive cavity walls filled with fine sand and gravel. The thatched roofs are cleverly aerodynamic to withstand the worst gales. Even so a cheerful blaze is one of the most deeply satisfying pleasures. Modern *Tirisdich* (native Tiree folk) have oil, coal and electricity to choose from but in days past they had to use whatever was available to them from the island. The meagre peat soon ran out and, with no wood to use, they had to look elsewhere, and so The Duke of Argyll allowed island men to sail, or row, the 20 miles to the neighbouring islands of Mull or Coll to cut peat supplies.

I sat, one late November afternoon, in *An Iodhlann*, the tiny museum on Tiree, listening to the wind and rain outside and talking to Catriona McLeod and Duncan Grant. Duncan is a keen local historian and was thrilled to have traced his great-grandfather, via the 1841 census, collecting peats on Mull. The Tiree men had been on Mull at the time of the census which reported up to 20 people staying in a house 'for the purpose of digging peat.' The open boats would be loaded with ballast stones on Tiree and they would be dumped on Mull to make room for the peats on the way back. Over the years there built up quite pile of discarded ballast on Mull, called *Clachan nan Tirisdich – The stones of the Tiree people*, which can still be seen today if you know where to look.

The early outsiders to visit these islands reported rude, windowless huts, milk and a few potatoes for food, and nothing but dried turf for fuel. Even Duncan Grant remembers being sent by his aunt during the war years to collect cattle dung for the fire. 'I would go out on a sunny day and turn them over to dry the other side, and then go back a few days later with a sack from the byre to collect them. They burn well but they don't last long.'

I love the stories of the hard men who trek the Hindu Kush and drink from puddles in their search for stories to bring us, and I do enjoy camping. Sometimes, however, I take my slippers and a few good books. I rent a modern, double-glazed cottage and I keep up to date with my emails. At the Co-op on Tiree I can buy European wines, Belgian chocolate, groceries and a lottery ticket. Even so I can still imagine the old ways. There is something primordial about walking along the strand line of an empty beach and collecting jetsam for kindling. It fulfils our human need to provide for ourselves at the most basic level that earning six figures in the City never could. The joy of such a walk is that, after filling my bag with wood, I can light my fire and sit in comfort, satisfied at having provided myself with cosy shelter for the night.

There is no light pollution on Tiree, save the illuminated signs on the Royal Bank of Scotland and the Co-op. They shine in a few

Scarinish bedroom windows, disturbing the blackness of the winter nights. Otherwise there is just the Moon and stars to guide you on your way home after dark. With a clear sky, and a full moon, the light reflecting off the wet, shiny black ribbon of single track road is more than enough to save you from stumbling into the ditch. At other times you might need the torch the landlady at the Scarinish Hotel will gladly lend you to see yourself safely home.

After dinner in Scarinish one evening I turned out into one of those calm clear nights, with big stars, when you just have to stop, and look, and take it all in, as the piper plays. The next time I walked the two miles back to my cottage it was a much wilder night, with wind blowing foam over the harbour wall and sand blasting from the beach to gather in the edge of the road. Incredibly, it seemed, a stoical heron was standing motionless in the water's edge and the local herring gull was stood, almost where I had left him three hours earlier, on the back lawn, eyes half closed, facing the gale.

Twice a year the island is visited by migrant birds, on passage to or from their breeding grounds. In the spring, especially in good weather, they rush north with all the vim and vigour of hormonally charged teenagers. In the autumn they amble back at a more sedate pace, with only New Year's Eve and the January sales to look forward to. Redwings were all over the island in November, heading south from breeding in Scandinavia. They would pass this way again in the spring, looking spruce in their freshly moulted breeding plumage.

Redwings joined flocks of lapwings, dotted about the short grass, having their crests tousled and stepping quickly to stay upright in the wind. The famous corncrakes have gone by autumn ('Get a corncrake on your croft and you can retire on the subsidies'. they say) but for whooper swans, Greenland white-fronted and barnacle geese Tiree is far enough south for them to over-winter.

The first gales litter the shores with rotting kelp or 'tangles' and grey seals haul out on the Atlantic skerries to pup. The kelp once helped feed the islanders, who waded in at low tide to harvest it for burning down to potash. Kelping must have been a freezing, toilsome trade, needing the stoicism of the heron or the gull. Now the washed up tangles feed only the sanderlings and dunlin that poke about it for invertebrates.

Caledonian MacBrayne's *Clansman* makes the four hour trip from Oban, via Coll, just three times a week at this time of year. In the summer there are sailings every day and the locals find that much easier. I was packed and ready to leave Tiree on the Thursday morning but the gale had returned and it looked as though I might be marooned until the weekend. In the event *Clansman* rocked up to the pier at Gott Bay and I went home, along with a few locals on Christmas shopping trips, and the bull who had been over on a busman's holiday.

A weather window gave us a smooth sail past the Treshnish Isles, Ardnamurchan and into the Sound of Mull. The boat was quiet without the chattering, grizzling hordes of August and I had the observation lounge almost to myself. The purple mountains with the last of the dun bracken were wreathed in slate grey cloud for as far as I could see. It was still early but already the lighthouses at Tobermory, Lismore and Lady's Rock pricked the gloaming. Duart castle, black and grey on its rock, slid past and I have never seen it looking more 'Lord of the Isles'.

Clansman heeled and turned for Oban and the reverie was shattered by the loud lady with a mobile phone, ordering a ton of gravel and some bricks from the builders' merchant. I don't suppose she knew what she had done.

CHAPTER 13

Skye – You can still go by ferry

LIKE THEM OR loathe them ferries are the corpuscles of island life. Islanders have a love/hate, relationship with them. They are given pet names such as Loti (Lord of the Isles) and St Roller (St Ola, the former northern isles vessel) I don't know if her sea-keeping qualities were poor or not. I suspect the snub stuck because it just happened to rhyme.

Islanders love to complain about the service they get from their local ferry companies. I once made the mistake of asking an island laird what time the boat arrived and was treated to a 30 minute tirade along the lines of '… what possible use are they? They run infrequently, deliver very little freight, at exorbitant rates and bring only people like you who spend very little money when you get here.' I think things are a better now. The island in question has since passed into community ownership.

When Gigha, a mile off the Kintyre peninsula, was bought out by the locals the government announced, on the day the deeds were handed over, that the ferry service would be more frequent, making the school run to the mainland easier for the children. This may have been opportunist making of political capital, a good soundbyte for the politician, but there is no doubt such things impact massively on whether young families choose to stay on islands or not. Ferries are, in fact, vital.

Way out in the North Sea, half way between Orkney and Shetland is Fair Isle, a rocky outpost with 70 people, many sheep and many more seabirds. Fair Islanders depend absolutely on their sole boat. Her name – *Good Shepherd IV* – reflects how spiritually bound they are to her, and how they feel about the service and protection she offers them.

When *Good Shepherd IV* leaves her slip at North Haven for the two and a half hours crossing to Grutness, on the southern tip of Shetland, the skipper has to be sure the weather will hold long enough for them to recover the boat onto her cradle upon their return five or six hours later. At least one trip back from Shetland ended in Orkney because they couldn't make Fair Isle in the gale – they just blew straight past.

A tiny community, of just 22 souls, lives on Foula, 20 miles west of the Shetland mainland. Winter storms can keep their boat – *New Advance* – shore bound for weeks at a time in some years. In any case she has to be hoisted high out of the water onto a concrete plinth after every trip, winter and summer such is the lack of protection from the Atlantic rollers that have thousands of miles to build up as they come from the Gulf of Mexico.

Caledonian MacBrayne operates ferries to 24 islands off the west coast of Scotland. In 2013 a new generation of diesel/electric, hybrid ferry boats is due to come into service. Cal Mac will take delivery of two new vessels, powered by electric motors that will be the first such roll on – roll off ferries in the world. The propellers will be powered by electric motors served by on-board diesel generators, so there will still be a need for conventional diesel fuel use.

The clever bit, however, is the inclusion of lithium-ion batteries that will deliver about 20 per cent of power (and hence 20 per cent fuel saving and emission reduction). The batteries will be re-charged over-night when the boat is alongside the pier. Ultimately the charge will come from wind, wave, tidal or solar power, making the operation even greener. Alternative energy sources are developing well in the islands – especially Orkney and Shetland – so, this is a genuine prospect.

The new hybrid boats will each carry 150 passengers and 23 cars or two heavy goods vehicles. If you are new to island going you might be amazed to see some of the very biggest articulated lorries rolling on and off some ferries carrying, among many other things, fish and shellfish to European markets.

The new boats will be suitable for short runs and the first service is likely to be the hop from Skye to Raasay. As the battery boats develop I hope we will see them on all the island piers. One of the real problems with the conventional ferries is the noise the generators make over-night. I have lain in my tent, by the pier or in a harbour-side B&B listening to the all-pervasive thrum of the boats as they lay – lit up like Christmas trees – all night. It seems a shame, when islands advertise 'peace and tranquillity' as a unique selling point, that everyone sleeping near the harbour must listen to the noise. Locals get used to it and will tolerate it because the ferry is vital to them but it will be much better for everyone when the boats hook up to the mains like caravans.

Ferries are, often, the single most important factor keeping an island open for trade. Islanders rely on telephone and computer engineers, vets, doctors, teachers and others to keep them open for business, and they all rely on the ferry.

Families cannot stay on small islands if there is no school provision. Sometimes there will be a small primary school with a handful of children but students may have to cross the water from very small islands to study – even at a very young age. In Orkney the boat leaves Tingwall, on the mainland, at 08.00 Monday to Friday. It calls at the island of Rousay 20 minutes later and picks up passengers for the even smaller islands of Wyre and Egilsay. If this is a school morning it will also collect someone charged with the important task of escorting primary school children. The chaperone makes the ten minute crossing to Wyre where she meets two primary children and escorts them back to Rousay for their school day. The boat is then free to sail, finally, for Egilsay (which has its own small school).

I took this boat from Tingwall one day in August, when school was closed, but we still made the double call at Rousay. No one got on. 'It's a scheduled service,' said the mate. 'We have to do it.' Looking back now I still can't quite understand why the service just doesn't have a little note next to it in the timetable that says 'Term time only'. However, let me not quibble. This is another example of the extraordinary lengths to which the islanders, their councils and ferry operators will go to keep the schools, businesses and families leading their modern lives.

The inter-island passenger service has come a long way since the first steamers exactly 200 years ago. In 2011 I travelled on the newly commissioned MV *Finlaggan* – Caledonian MacBrayne's new boat for the Islay run. I joined ship at Port Askaig early one morning after camping on Jura for a few days. Luxury is always more appreciated after a period of roughing it.

I watched from the rail as the last of the vehicles came aboard and the ramp was raised. The lines were cast off and *Finlaggan* became, for a couple of hours, an island in her own right. It was a cold, early morning so I went inside and closed the tight-fitting outer door.

The atmosphere inside was warm and unbelievably quiet after the older boats I was used to. I explored the amenities and then enjoyed a long, hot shower before going in for a full Scottish breakfast. The forward cafeteria has one particular improvement on earlier ferries: I could sit at my table and enjoy panoramic views over the hills of Jura and Islay. It was low season so I had a table to myself at which to enjoy my mariner's fare. The blue and white saltire fluttered briskly and noislessly at the prow.

The fantastic range of greens, browns and purples on the hillside stood out against the cold grey of the sea and sky. It is lovely to enjoy the islands from the comfort of the ship. You glide past long, trackless headlands that would take days to penetrate on foot. If you've been camping, walking, cycling or kayaking you certainly feel deserving of this treat. After the breakfast comes the hot coffee and the view rolls on. Maybe a few gobs of rain or spray hit the window and intensify the feeling of a stolen pleasure.

Friends often cite the weather as a reason for not visiting Scotland. How little they know. The weather is a very good reason to go. If you don't like the weather at any particular moment, no matter, just wait five minutes. You can often get all four seasons in a morning. Then again there will be whole days of deep blue, cloudless skies, calm blue seas, gaily painted fishing boats and sparkling lighthouses, on verdant headlands, casting sharp shadows as you pass. If such a day comes after a week of clag you will treasure the memory for ever.

The sound between the islands of Jura and Islay widened and, cruising at over 16 knots, we were soon at Kennacraig on the mainland, but not before I'd had an hour's deep, warm sleep in a luxuriously upholstered reclining seat.

MV *Finlaggan* is a direct descendent of PS *Comet* – launched in 1812 by a Mr Henry Bell. The *Comet* was the first Clyde steamship, a paddle steamer. Railways arrived in 1840 and, gradually, the small steamship companies were taken over by bigger concerns. In 1851 David and Alexander Hutcheson joined with David MacBrayne to form the basis of the fleet that operates today. The packet company became the part nationalised Caledonian MacBrayne (Cal Mac) in 1973 and passed into the sole ownership of the Scottish government in 2000.

A competition had been held on Islay to find a name for their new boat. In spirit, if not in law, the boats are very much the property of the islanders. *Finlaggan* is a tiny loch, with a tiny island, in the centre of Islay. 500 years ago the lords of the isles lived and held their councils here. Today the causeway from the visitor centre leads across the shallow, reedy loch to the few remaining stone ruins. From Finlaggan the lords dispensed government and justice to the vast island regions of the west. They ruled an almost independent kingdom – Scotland's Island Country – until King James IV became tired of this thorn in his side and dispossessed them.

It is often said that Scotland is a land of myth and legend. History scholars have difficulty in separating fact from fiction when looking at the past. Wherever the truth lies there can be little doubt about the significance and affection in which the old heroes are still held in Scotland. Bonnie Prince Charlie, Robert the Bruce, Mary Queen of Scots, William Wallace and John – Lord of the Isles.

Ferries to the island of Lewis, in the Outer Hebrides, are as vital to the islands sustainability as they are anywhere else. They are a long way from the mainland, have a large population (22,000) and the air link is very expensive. There have been deep divisions in the island community, however, over the decision taken in 2009 to start operating a Sunday service from the mainland.

Writing in *The Guardian* in May 2009 Ian Jack said 'Lewis is probably the last place in Europe where Christianity can dictate the pattern of everyday life.' The staunchly Presbyterian majority on Lewis, and the adjoining island of Harris, are devotees of the fourth commandment and seek to keep the Sabbath holy. This they interpret as no gardening, no hanging out washing and certainly no ferries.

In former days members of the clergy have lain down on ferry slip ways to prevent landings when the ruling had been challenged. As with communities everywhere else, however, the Lord's Day observance had been gradually eroded before the first Sunday boat in 2009. People drove their cars, a few pubs and restaurants opened and council workers came out early to clear away the broken glass and vomit left over from Saturday night. Ferries had arrived 'by the back door' via Harris from North Uist on Sundays since 2006 and flights had been sneaking into Stornoway airport since 2002 on the Sabbath.

Love them or loathe them? In the end I think they are actually very much loved. A small group of community activists refused to bow to the inevitable when the Skye road bridge opened in 1995. The ferry should, logically, have been consigned to history. There are even those who refuse to accept Skye as an island since it has a fixed link. The Glenelg to Skye ferry (*Glenahulish*) continues to serve this most iconic of Scottish islands during the summer months however.

The *Glenahulish* is the last remaining manually operated turntable ferry in Scotland. The boat pulls alongside a concrete slipway and the crew manually haul the six-car turntable deck round so cars can drive on and off over the side. The crossing is advertised as 'the traditional way to Skye' and enough tourists are moved to keep the service alive. It takes just five minutes to go over the sea to Skye.

In 2013, a new service from Ardrossan to Campbeltown, on the southern tip of Kintyre (near the Mull of Kintyre) was announced. Of course, not everyone was happy: 'They will be at the wrong times, on the wrong days, and at the wrong price,' someone said. 'They will take money out of Campbeltown, rather than bringing it in. Ach well.'

CHAPTER 14

Outer Hebrides – Hitch-hiking with a ballerina

'THE BACK OF BEYOND' and 'The Outer Hebrides' used to be synonymous when wanting to convey the idea of utter remoteness and absolute inaccessibility and I suppose this is still the view held by many today. In fact the islands (also known as The Western Isles or The Long Island) can be reached in under an hour by plane from Glasgow or about five hours by boat from Oban. Of course for those with the 'Island Madness', the remoteness of islands is part of the addiction for which there is no known cure – and only one treatment – to go there.

To draw a quick mental map of the Outer Hebrides imagine a ballerina standing *en pointe*. Lewis, the largest and most northerly isle, will form the thigh, and tiny Berneray, 130 miles south, will be the toe tip on which she is standing. North Uist in the middle points a rather unflattering, knobbly knee west, out into Atlantic and there you are. The toe is dipped into the water about 40 miles west of the Scottish mainland. You are now ready to place any of the 50-odd islands in their geographical context.

Hilly in places, but not mountainous, the highest point is Clisham on Lewis which, at 2,600ft, falls short of qualification as a Munro by some 400ft. The Western Isles are largely tree-less today although, like most of Britain, they were densely wooded until a thousand years or so ago. The forests were cleared by islanders and Viking marauders alike, and once they were gone it became very difficult to re-establish them. A sapling needs a forest around it to shelter it from the wind.

There is a rich legacy of peat on the islands and this has been utilised by islanders for a large part of the 5,000 years of their continuous occupation (There are archaeological sites which point to this occupation of which perhaps the most striking are the stones of Callanish on the west side of Lewis, erected about 4,000 years ago).

Peat has, in fact, become associated with Scotland by people the world over. During this trip through the Long Island in the '90s I met a delightful young American couple who had been living, alone, in the restored Black House Gatliff Trust hostel at Garenin for three days prior to my arrival. It was a cold spring and, as the young man heaped more coal on the stove, he turned to me and said 'This *is* peat isn't it?' Sadly, the Garenin hostel is now closed but there are still three, simple Gatliff hostels in the Outer Hebrides.

There are beaches to die for. It is rarely hot at this latitude, but on clear, bright blue sunny days the sands are as fine and dramatically beautiful as any in the world. The climate conspires with the legendary midges to keep tourism to a level far below that of Spain or the Caribbean, but for those that make it here (May and June are the best times to visit) the vistas and sunsets will sear the soul like no other.

The Western Isles are a modern, thriving community which makes its living from fishing and farming principally. The fisherman find their way to the fish with global positioning systems, fish finders, radar and navigation software that would not be out of place in a space ship. Businesses ashore are computerised and Stornoway teenagers text each other as frequently and as inconsequentially as youngsters in any European town. So, if we mistake remoteness for lack of progress we do so at our peril, but the modernity of the Hebrides is set in a timeless and unchanging landscape that allows us to see the islands almost as they were generations ago. The wooden piers and gaily painted corrugated iron roofs have almost gone but I hitch-hiked along with the thought that I may be Boswell or even Johnson himself.

I had flown into Stornoway – the commercial capital town of about 8,000 people and, after a couple of nights camping on the edge of town waiting for the Sabbath to pass I set off to hitch-hike out of town on the main road south.

After a short wait I was picked up by the mobile shopkeeper, in his mobile shop and sat on the fish box, where the passenger seat should have been, for the two hours or so it took to visit Mrs McLeod, Mrs McNeil, Mrs MacFadyan, Mrs MacDonald, Katie Morag and Mrs Smith. Eventually we pulled into his home where his wife was waiting to serve us a sumptuous breakfast of eggs, bacon and all the local trimmings.

We carried on south and it took the rest of the morning to reach

Tarbert, where Lewis becomes Harris. After a cup of coffee in Tarbert I walked back up the road to the mountain track which heads off towards the small coastal community of Rhenigidale to find the second of the Gatliff Trust hostels and a bed for the night. *Country Life* magazine has described this hill path as one of the finest walks in the land and I cannot disagree. Although the tops were white with snow the walk was warming enough, with East Loch Tarbert behind me I walked across the headland overlooking Scalpay, to reach the sea again at Loch Tollamarig and then round the coast to Rhenigidale beside Loch Seaforth.

Rhenigidale was reputed to be the remotest community in Britain until the road was completed about 25 years ago. Hostel warden, Roddy McInnes had campaigned for the road but sadly died in 1986, just before its completion. Roddy is buried in the cemetery at Maaruig, close by the road.

The following day I backtracked along the coast and turned down to the sea at Molinginish, one of the many deserted fishing and crofting hamlets to be found all over the islands. This one was having new life breathed into it however, two of the houses had fine new roofs and were being fitted out as, I guessed, away-from-it-all holiday homes – boat access only.

A notice in the hostel said 'Taxi to phone box – £2'; I paid a bit extra and had a ride to Tarbert in the morning and then down the road for the ferry to Scalpay (we're coming down the back of the thigh to the knee just now, by the way). They were just building a bridge to Scalpay when I was there – it was still an island then so I popped over on the flit boat and camped by the harbour for the night.

The following day I made it down to Leverburgh from where I would later catch the ferry across the Sound of Harris to North Uist. In the meantime I went into the post office for a few tourist items and was invited to join them for a mug of tea (it is the many kindnesses, such as the ride in the shop, the breakfast and the invitation to tea in the post office that I remember, and treasure as the real souvenirs of my visit).

I had plenty of time before the ferry so I left my rucksack at the pier and legged it down to have a look at St Clement's church at Rodel, at the southern tip of Harris. I followed the instructions on the door and collected the key from the house to have a look round inside this most beautiful of buildings. In my mind's eye (and in my camera) I had to edit out the little bit of scaffolding on the tower.

There followed two of the most exquisite camp-sites ever. On Berneray, across the Sound of Harris, I pitched by the beach and enjoyed a swim (wash) before a good meal cooked on the camp stove (rice and assorted tinned meals are sold in all island shops and are very handy for one-pan cooking).

After tea there was a brisk walk up to look at the Gatliff hostel in the north of the island – another lovely, restored black house that I often see featured in postcards. The following night I was back on North Uist and camping by the beach at Hougharry. After warming up to a crackling driftwood fire on the sand, I fell asleep around midnight. This was corncrake country but it was still a bit too early in the season for them.

I carried on heading south in the morning (down the shin) and it was a slow process as no-one seems to drive very far in the islands and I was relying on lifts that day. There are a few places left where I feel comfortable hitch-hiking, and where the locals are happy to pass the time of day with visitors who aren't in a hurry. The following, short transcripts are of conversations enjoyed on a succession of short lifts. They were a real joy and offered sound-bites of local life:

'Will you take a cup of tea?' Lady going to do chores for her mum – three miles.

'My wee brother, Rory, wishes he had an island named after him.' Rona (aged five) and her dad – three miles.

'Why do you come here?' TV repair man – ten miles

'I hit a deer the other day, I hid it in the heather until dark then we came back with a saw and cut it in half – it's best boiled with mutton to give it flavour.' An old farmer and a dog – five miles.

'It's my first day on the island. It's not as bad as I thought, they told me the rain would be coming down sideways.' An army type from the Benbecula rocket range – five miles

'Why on Earth do you come here?' Seaweed dealer – five miles

'The army is just a big boys club' Old lady – three miles

I made it to Howmore Gatliff hostel by late afternoon and bagged a bed in the annexe (shed). Disturbed by a tawny owl at midnight I got up and looked out over snow-capped hills, lit by the biggest moon you ever saw. I do not believe you can buy moments like this at any price.

Arsenal was playing Blackburn Rovers on the TV in the public bar of the Lochboisdale hotel the following night when I walked up after pitching my tent by the pier. The lads were in, still celebrating Saturday's old firm win by Glasgow Rangers. This was Monday – the bar tender said they had been home, briefly, for something to eat on Sunday so I joined them to watch the match before turning in.

There were soon chants of 'Dougie, Dougie' and a lad I took to be Dougie jumped up on a table and proceeded to do a traditional Scottish dance. He danced from table to table, knocking over ash trays. Dougie was hardly disturbing anyone. There was only me and an old man of about eighty in the bar and he sat in the corner sipping his pint in a quiet, reserved 'I've seen all this before' sort of manner. Everywhere I went people were offering me something to eat or drink and here was no exception – Dougie finished his performance and bought drams for me and the old fellow.

I shook the sheets of ice from the tent in the morning and wandered up to see what time the hotel opened for breakfast, it was only 7am but the cook was just arriving for her shift and she let me in by the side door and I sat luxuriating in the warmth of the lounge and tucking into a gorgeous out-of-hours breakfast. The moon was just setting over the harbour.

Down at the ankle now I rode the ferry from the tip of South Uist as she rocked and rolled all the way across to Eoligarry on Barra (quite definitely at the foot of the islands.) The land was running out. I got a lift into Castlebay with a van load of shellfish divers. They spend two and a half hours a day in the water collecting razor shells, which they sell to the Spanish market. 'Would you like a cup of tea?' they asked when we got to their shed.

Castlebay is dominated by Kiessimul[1] castle which stands on a rock in the bay. I was looking at the castle, and wondering if it would repay a visit, when an old man appeared by my side and announced: 'Lived here all my life and never been in it – I'm not a McNeil you see, so that's my excuse.' He was telling me how life was better in the old days. 'They used to show films in the hall but I don't think they bother any more – everyone has TV and video these days, although I don't have one myself.' We leant on a rail and talked some more of this and that and the passing of the old ways. At length he departed as suddenly as he had come, taking his leave with 'Excuse me just now, I must away and get my lottery ticket.'

Castlebay is almost as near as you can get to the ballerina's toe without a special charter. Sandray, Pabbay, Mingulay and Berneray would all have to wait until another time. They are an itch that refuses to be scratched – along with the Monachs to the west and Shiants to the East. When you think you've got to the end of the land, and you look out to sea, there's always a bit more waiting to be explored. And when you get there you will, likely as not, find a half tumbled wall, or a gable end standing as a monument to a past tenancy. People have always wanted to go and see what it's like over there – and so do I.

Note

1 Kiessimul is also, sometimes, spelt 'Kissimul' or even 'Chisimul'. Spellings of Gaelic words translated into English are always a problem and tend to be primarily phonetic.

Kiessimul Castle, Barra

CHAPTER 15

Vatersay – Not a deserted island

ONE HUNDRED YEARS AGO the tiny Hebridean island of Mingulay, near the southern tip of the Outer Hebrides, was abandoned when the last family left for a new croft in nearby Vatersay. Islanders had, one by one, closed their doors and simply sailed away, leaving houses and furniture behind. In 2012 a mass was said on the island to mark the centenary of evacuation.

Mingulay had become impossible. There remained too few able bodied men to handle the boat. More productive land was available on Vatersay, nearer to Barra, so islanders moved for a better life. They didn't all want to go but, in the end, knew they had to.

Of 165 Scottish islands 60 are inhabited today and I can find approximate dates for the abandonment of 54 others over the last 200 years. I assume people have lived on them all if we look back far enough.

Famously abandoned islands such as Mingulay and St Kilda, 40 miles further west, were continuously inhabited for 5,000 years or so. They were home to small, contented communities who never thought of moving.

They were self-sufficient in food, clothing, building materials and fuel. In recent centuries they produced a surplus which was paid to landlords as rent. Gradually, as contact with the outside world increased through chance encounters with fishing boats and the early tourists on steamers, islanders began to imagine greener pastures. At first it was youngsters leaving for career opportunities then older folk left because they could no longer manage on their own.

Governments and landlords are not famous for their concern for islanders. Humanitarian aid would sometimes be forthcoming during crises but little else was done to support communities. In 1885, for instance, St Kildans lost their boat and some crops in a storm so sent one of the famous St Kilda Mailboats. Messages were enclosed in wooden 'boats' and cast into the sea. The 'mailboats' reached the Outer Hebrides within two weeks and relief supplies were sent. After that the islanders were left to their own devices again.

Today's administrators have a much more sympathetic view of islanders, and greater determination to help sustain and develop island living. 'There is a commitment to peripherality.' according to some council jargon.

In the west, the government-owned Caledonian Macbrayne provides heavily subsidised ferries for 24 islands. A new, £8m 'hybrid' (diesel/electric) boat has been commissioned to ply between Skye (population 9,232) and Raasay (population 192). In Orkney and Shetland the local councils operate boats between most inhabited islands and the central 'mainlands'.

Primary schools are kept open for tiny numbers of children and this encourages young families to remain or even move to the islands. Out Skerries in Shetland (population 85) maintains a secondary department in its school for as few as two students in some years. On Ewe, in the Western Isles, four children were sailed across each day and bussed on a round trip to school of 26 miles so they could be brought up as islanders which their parents believed was of sufficient value to justify the journey.

When Fetlar, Shetland, (population 47) was found to be struggling in 2007, councillors and locals rallied to form a working group. Empty houses were renovated, wireless broadband was laid on and a breakwater for the ferry constructed. Now, more people can live in Fetlar (population in 2013 – 71) and either work at home using the internet or commute to Yell or Kirkwall (the breakwater – completed in 2012 – means the ferry can lie at the island overnight for an early morning crossing).

Transport links between tiny islands and larger centres are probably the key to maintaining viability. In recent years fixed links (bridges and causeways) have been provided to a number of communities.

Perhaps the most famous link is the Skye bridge, opened in 1995 as a private finance initiative but toll-free since 2004. A bridge has also been provided over the narrows between Scalpay and Harris (opened in 1997). Causeways have been built to Berneray from North Uist (1998), Vatersay from Barra (1991) and Eriskay from South Uist (2001).

Vatersay had provided a home to evacuated islanders from Mingulay but when it too began to suffer declining population the link was established. Some locals complained it spoiled their island way of life: 'We have to lock our doors now,' was one complaint.

So keen were the Vatersay folk to use the causeway, however, that they regularly crossed in landrovers before the tarmac was laid. They may have to lock their doors but few would demolish the link now. It has provided better access to social services, refuse collection, jobs, shops, a daily post and tourism potential. These are the things that keep islands open.

Vatersay population fluctuations

1901	13	Following 19th century clearances
1912	288	After Mingulay and other folk settled
1971	77	20th century decline
1981	107	After local authority houses built
1988	65	After still more left for pastures new
2001	83	Causeway saves the island – at least for now.

The Churchill Barriers, linking the southern Orkney islands of South Ronaldsay, Burray, Glims Holm and Lamb Holm to the Orkney Mainland – were built during World War II. They were commissioned to protect Scapa Flow from enemy submarines, following the devastating attack which sank HMS *Royal Oak*. The barriers today allow people to reach Orkney in 45 minutes from John O'Groats then drive to Kirkwall in half an hour.

There has even been talk of a tunnel from Orkney to the Scottish mainland, possibly using the deserted (in 1961) island of Stroma as a stepping stone. The cost is prohibitive but if Orkney continues to market itself as 'The Energy Island – World Capital of Marine Renewables' then who knows? The world's renewable energy industry might just beat a path across (or under) the Pentland Firth. A tunnel would also be a handy conduit for fibre optic, broadband cable and the much needed extra power cables – to export renewable energy.

A £70m, fixed causeway between Orkney's Westray (population 563) and Papa Westray (population 65) was mooted a few years ago but quietly shelved. It would have enabled folk on the smaller island to access leisure and social amenities on Westray but you can't please everyone. Some people live on Papa Westray for the 'away-from-it-all-ness' and so opposed the link. Incidentally, the two islands share a Guinness Book of Records entry for the world's shortest scheduled air service (officially two minutes). When I took the flight a few years ago we hopped from one grassy field to another in seconds, when the door opened a sheep dog jumped in to see who was passing.

There are difficult choices to be made when supporting small communities at the expense of larger centres. The debate is ever-present in places such as Stornoway, Kirkwall and Lerwick. If a council spends money keeping an island open for business it may cost even more maintaining the school. It might be cheaper, sometimes, just to fund the evacuation.

It is not impossible, however, that 100 Scottish islands have been abandoned in the last few centuries. We should not want an ocean full of 'ghost islands' anchored round our shores, where no bright-funnelled ferries sail. With wind and wave and tidal energy, broadband and broad shoulders, islands can remain open for business and young islanders can lead modern lives.

CHAPTER 16

Mingulay – The ballerina's toe

LOTS OF PEOPLE dream of being Robinson Crusoe. The appeal of solitude on a small island is hard to explain but, if you have felt it, you will understand. In my Christmas stocking last year was a copy of Judith Schalansky's excellent *Atlas of Remote Islands*. The book is subtitled: *Fifty Islands I have not visited and never will*. Shalansky's book takes us to the remotest places on Earth, including Christmas Island, Easter Island, Lonely Island in the Arctic and Bouvet Island in the Southern Ocean. The inclusion of our own St Kilda reminds us of just what a special place we have on our doorstep, and not nearly so difficult to visit as the others.

Scotland has, depending on your definition, around 160 offshore islands and several of them can offer a Crusoe experience for those prepared to make a little effort. There are a few basic requirements to human comfort that can make a stay on an uninhabited island a deeply satisfying sojourn as opposed to a wet and miserable trial. My own list of needs is very short: a warm, dry shelter in which I can stand up; somewhere flat to sleep; hot food and drink; a chair in which to sit and read – or doze – some candles; peace and quiet and solitude. There are a few places where you can get this, and little else.

I sailed from Oban to Barra on Caledonian MacBrayne's MV *Lord of The Isles* one beautiful June morning. Travelling alone increases one's chance of interesting encounters and my first was with 12 students travelling to Castlebay for their own, private, weekend 'beer festival'. They were delightful lads and I became their hero when I helped them with their tent, which they had been attempting to erect inside out. Later we shared a table in the hotel bar as local band, the *Vatersay Boys*, hammered out their unique brand of folk rock late into the night.

Our rough campsite by the shore was very quiet in the early morning so I packed and crept away. Donald McLeod picked me up from the harbour in his boat – *Boy James* – for the hour's crossing to Mingulay – the largest of the group, known as the Bishop's

Isles, just south of Barra. On the way we passed Vatersay, Muldoanich, Sandray and Pabbay.

We arrived off the pristine white sand beach of Mingulay Bay, half way down the east side of the island and directly below the old village. The air was thick with puffins from the colony, a quarter of a million strong, on slopes just to the north. *Boy James* anchored in the bay and I swam ashore while Donald ferried my gear in the dingy.

Mingulay was bought by The National Trust for Scotland in 2000 and a single building in the village, the schoolhouse, has been restored and re-roofed to provide bothy accommodation for NTS workers. Donald very kindly lent me the key so I had everything on my list of basic Crusoe needs. I had even shipped a bag of house coal, as June evenings can be cold out there in the Atlantic.

I collected sparkling, clean fresh water from the burn running down past the house. It is amazing how much one can use for just cooking, washing up, washing a few clothes and personal ablutions. Ten gallons, easily, in a day. There was a container in the house, a scoop and a lovely flat stone in a deep pool where the burn meandered past a display of marigolds.

I settled in, stacked my rations on the dresser, books on the mantelpiece and went for a walk. These old Hebridean houses have small windows so I lit a couple of candles in late afternoon and sat with a dram. The Islay single malt wasn't on my list of essentials but I had smuggled a bottle of Laphroaig across anyway. Later I lit a coal fire and cooked up some rice and meatballs on the meths stove. A tin of rice pudding with added peach slices made my traditional bothy dessert.

A couple more candles gave a soft, warm light and fantastic ambience. The thick walls kept out what little sound there was from the wind. Only the shrill oystercatchers made themselves heard from outside. I settled into the armchair and ran through my checklist: replete, dry, warm, comfortable and quiet. I could stare into the fire, gaze out of the window or read for as long as I wished. The only trouble with such comfort and contentment is that I am often soon asleep. I was woken around midnight by corncrakes rasping outside and didn't mind a bit. There was a trace of light still in the sky, as there often is at these latitudes in spring. Shetlanders call it the 'simmer dim'.

In the morning, after breakfast on the patio, I wandered down the grassy track to the remains of the old village. The schoolhouse is set apart from the village, on a raised plateau and with generous, enclosed gardens. Its builders clearly wanted to afford the teacher some of the comfort and seclusion they felt his status deserved. Only one or two gables remain standing in the village as most houses are reduced to rings of stones, half filled with blown sand. In the graveyard a few, crude crosses are still poking through.

The community on Mingulay went the way of so many others. Famously, St Kilda survived until 1930 but by 1912 Mingulay was deserted. With no safe harbour and too few able bodied men to haul boats in and out through the surf they could not continue.

Islanders had started to travel and see a better life for themselves elsewhere. Many were resettled on Vatersay where more land was available nearer to the stronger community on Barra. More recently even Vatersay has needed a causeway to survive. Small island communities are romantic notions but I support the bridge builders every time if they provide a life line. Berneray, Scalpay and Eriskay in the Western Isles have all been given concrete connections during my island hopping days. There will still be enough quiet places for us to go and ponder.

We tend to romanticise small island places, believing they hold answers to our modern, hectic lives – they do not. You can sit quietly and contemplate turquoise seas, pure, white sand and flawless *machair* to the horizon for as long as you like but they will not cure anything in you. At best you will see yourself reflected exactly as you are. You might feel your own strengths and weaknesses. In the extreme solitude you might realise that you have, actually, an inner strength that allows you to be alone. Or you might want to hurry back to urban clamour. Whichever is the case you will be a little wiser.

On my last morning on Mingulay I was tidying the bothy and packing my few things. The sun was streaming in through the open door and skylarks were trilling away outside. I didn't want to be leaving really but Donald had said a storm was coming (I've fallen for that one before. These island boatmen often invoke an imminent gale when what they really mean is that it will be more convenient for them to move you today. Still, you have to trust the skippers – they will always get you there and back safely and that's the main thing).

There came a confident knock on the door and I looked up to see a gang of teenage girls, complete with strappy tops and skimpy shorts, standing outside in the sun. 'Can we have a look in your house, please?' The leader asked as they stepped inside. 'Can we have a look upstairs?' she said, as they trooped, single file, up the uncarpeted stairs. They were clumping about on the bare boards in the two small rooms above and I shouted up to be careful as the floor was rotten in places.

'Girls, you are more than welcome to look round, but didn't your mothers ever say anything to you about going into houses with strange men?' I asked. 'Ach, you look safe enough to us,' someone shouted down. Inspection over, they came down and explained that they were from Barra High School, this was 'Activity Day' and their 'activity' was fishing with Donald McLeod. Donald had dropped them off to have a look round Mingulay.

The Barra girls were supremely confident, well-spoken and good conversationalists. They told me the Queen had once landed from *Britannia* for a picnic and had sat in my very chair. As a former schoolteacher from Sheffield, it was interesting for me to note these students wearing the same fashions and having 'Activity Days' just the same – well, not quite the same – they were fishing off Mingulay instead of serving in WH Smiths.

Donald picked me off the beach at Mingulay Bay and we sailed 'south about' past Barra Head. The rare calm sea allowed *Boy James* passage through the arch at *Gunamul* and the chasm of *Arnamul* in the south west cliffs of Mingulay. 'Look. There's a basking shark,' said the skipper as we emerged into the sunlight below *Biulacraig*. And there was. On second thoughts, perhaps these places do have the power to heal.

The author enjoying some solitude, Mingulay.

CHAPTER 17

Mingulay – Perfect monsters

I COULD HEAR IN Gary Latter's voice the disappointment when I told him you could now get a mobile phone signal from the top of Mingulay. 'That changes things,' he said. As a rock climber he rates Mingulay and Pabbay among the very best rock climbing in the UK and one of the attractions for the serious climber is the commitment and isolation required to climb there. Even a phone signal diminishes that slightly.

Gary and his climbing partners will make up a party of 12 to fill Donald McLeod's boat – *Boy James* – and have him leave them on Mingulay for a week to camp and climb the sheer, sea girt cliffs that make up almost the whole of the west side of the island. Donald will call back half way through their stay and move them to Pabbay, for a change of scene and some different climbs, but Gary often prefers to stay on Mingulay because, as he says: 'There are plenty of routes and I don't want to waste a day moving camp when I could be on one of them.'

Mingulay is owned by the National Trust for Scotland and their suggested camp site for climbers is down on the flat, grassy plateau overlooking the beach, just south of the old village. From there it's a hike up the hill with all the gear for the climbing. The beauty of Mingulay is that you can leave all your heavy gear at the cliff top for the whole week – no one will steal it.

Each ascent begins at the top of the cliff. There is no access at the bottom so climbers must start by abseiling down. The fixed, 300 ft static rope for the abseil then remains in place as an emergency escape route. Climbing back up it is not a favoured option, however, as it can chafe and wear on rocky outcrops.

Gary and his partners, Twid Turner and Louise Thomas, pioneered a new route on Mingulay in 1995 which they called 'Perfect Monsters'. In the south west corner of the island is a headland called *Dun Mingulay* ending in the sheer cliff of *Sron a Duin* (Fortress Promontory). There, on the very westernmost tip of the island, they threw their rope into the abyss. The first attempt was aborted very quickly when the westerly gale threw the rope back up and deposited it in a tangled heap at their feet. Lesser mortals, myself included, would have grasped the excuse to head back to camp and put the kettle on. Gary, Twid and Louise simply walked round to find a cliff face out of the wind and went back to *Sron a Duin* later.

These guys need the rock to be dry for safe climbing so they will wait until the sun has moved round to the west to dry it before attempting anything tricky. At 3,700 million year–old, the rock (Lewisian gneiss) isn't going anywhere, so there's no hurry.

They finally set off to climb at 8pm on 21 June 2001. Gary led the first pitch and climbed about 80 ft before pausing at a good stance for his partner to come up. The leader of each pitch puts protection in place as he goes – to save himself from a dangerous fall and also for his partner to use, and then remove, as he comes up. Protection is usually an aluminium nut or cam with a rope loop on it. The cam goes in a crack in the rock, in such a way as to bear the weight of the climber when he pulls down on it, and the climbing rope passes through the loop. The climber will then climb a few feet past the cam before placing another. If he falls then the rope will catch him just below the last, fixed cam – provided his partner is awake and remembers to pull on the other end.

In the early evening the rock glows pink and gold in the setting sun. The next land west of *Sron a Duin*, apart from St Kilda, is Canada and the climbers felt the sun on their backs as it sank all the way to the horizon. Their only company was the two small sea-stacks called the Twin Rocks and the seabirds nesting on the cliffs. Guillemots, razorbills, kittiwakes and fulmars use the most precarious of ledges but, luckily, there aren't many on *Sron a Duin* as it is too steep and sheer even for them.

This was a difficult climb, finally graded overall as E7 with the hardest move a 6b. They managed two pitches (about 150 ft) before dark, then marked the spot and went up the safety rope. They abseiled back down the next day and took up where they had left off, completing this first ascent in 4 pitches and two days. The cliff overhangs at the top so it was not easy at the end.

Climbers use terms such as M for moderate; H for hard, D for difficult and so on. E stands for Extremely Severe – the highest grade – and E7 refers to a sub grade of which there are 11. I know about severe frosts, severe storms and severe bouts of flu so I can only imagine an E7 climb.

Gary, Louise and Twid called the route 'Perfect Monsters' after a line in an otherwise forgotten poem: 'Perfect monsters are bred on cliffs and crags'.

Lucy Creamer is one of the UK's top female climbers. I came to seek her out because of something I saw, and something Donald said, as we sailed back from Mingulay, down the west side of Pabbay. The skipper pointed out a huge arch in the face of the gigantic cliff. It was like a 300ft high fireplace hewn from the rock. The left hand vertical recess and the roof were in shadow and the whole structure stood on sea-washed boulders where the hearth should be. 'People come and try to climb that,' said Donald. Everyone on the boat was left speechless as we tried to come to terms with just how anyone could attempt such a feat.

Lucy is a professional climber. She makes her living these days from writing, running courses and instructing. She told me of the sacrifices she has made to follow her desire to be climbing, somewhere in the world, as often as possible. 'I do without the things many people take for granted. I don't have a mortgage and I drive beaten up cars but I have no regrets,' she said. 'I have done all sorts of work at times to pay for my addiction. I'll do a rope-access contract for a bit and pile up enough money to go off to Yosemite or somewhere,' she added.

'The Great Arch on Pabbay came about in an odd, round about sort of way,' Lucy said. 'We were sitting in a Chalet in Switzerland. It was a wet, miserable day, the climbing was off and we had found some videos. Things looked up a bit when we discovered they were climbing videos and we watched how a team had climbed The Great Arch on an island in The Outer Hebrides called Pabbay. It wasn't a free climb. The film makers had used various aid devices and rest points, over several days, to assist as they went and, of course, had the added problem of filming.' On an impulse Lucy decided to see if she could put together a group to go and make a first, free ascent. The American outdoor clothing company, Marmot, who sponsor Lucy and other British climbers, funded the Pabbay expedition for the whole group.

Lucy and her climbing partner, Steve McClure, actually came to Pabbay for a week and were the first to free climb The Great Arch – up the wall, across the roof (upside down – like a spider), out at the front of the roof (where the mantle clock would be on a fireplace) and up to the top of the cliff. They spent the first few days climbing some established routes and did the Great Arch towards the end. They did it in one day.

I had asked Lucy what they did on the islands when they weren't climbing. 'If it's raining we might chill in the mess tent with a book, or go for a walk on a rest day, although we pretty much climb all the time if we can. We are addicted after all,' she said.

Lucy has led a bohemian lifestyle. The climbing is the thing that fulfils her, not the acquisition of material things. She works to live and some of her best living has been on the stacks and sea cliffs of Scotland – the more remote the better.

Climbers of the calibre of Lucy Creamer and Gary Latter are tough, strong, single minded athletes. They are not risk takers or reckless thrill seekers but serious professionals. The image we sometimes have of them, hanging upside down from a roof or overhang, hundreds of feet above the waves crashing on the rocks below is one of incredible daring and of life hanging by a thread. The climbers that go to Mingulay, Pabbay and such places are the very best, however, and the challenges they set for themselves have been worked towards over many years of practice on lesser routes and climbing walls. 'It's as dangerous as you want to make it,' said Lucy.

It was lovely speaking to Gary and Lucy about the islands. I had expected climbers with eyes only for the routes but they were much more in touch with their souls than that. Gary's sadness at learning of mobile phone signals gave him away but he went on to enthuse about much more. 'There are birds and flowers all over the island,' he said. 'You can set off from London and be climbing in California quicker than you could be on Mingulay, but nowhere beats the isolation, the grandeur and the sunsets on Mingulay.' He also waxed lyrical about climbing on Eigg and Hoy but, as he gets too old and stiff to climb, the memories of beach campfires on Mingulay and the knowledge he was the first on *Perfect Monsters* will keep him warm at night.

'Mingulay and Pabbay offer some of the best rock climbing in the world,' said Lucy. 'Rock climbing has taken me to some fabulously beautiful, tranquil, secret places,' she added. 'The colour and texture of the rock in the evening sunlight is stunning and you rarely get that kind of peace in which to immerse yourself for the challenges of the climb anywhere else.'

Peel away the hard, glamorous image and they all say the same things about the remotest islands. They are fantastic places. There is splendid isolation, peace, tranquillity and beauty all around.

Climber, Mingulay.

CHAPTER 18

Shiant islands – Compton Mackenzie's islands

THE SHIANT ISLANDS are difficult to visit unless you have your own boat. There is no air or ferry service as they are tiny and uninhabited. Licensed boat charter operators will charge anything up to £500 return for the few miles of sea crossing from Stornoway. This is to cover the cost of the gas guzzling, fast RIBS and the loss of the day's fishing. You might be able to negotiate a better deal with a local fisherman, perhaps from Scalpay. Group bookings work out cheaper per head but then I wanted to go and experience the solitude of living alone in Compton Mackenzie's old bothy on *Tigh an Eilean*. The main island of the group of three is the only one that ever had a house on it. I had arranged with the owner, Adam Nicolson, to borrow the key to the house and spend a few days of peace and quiet.

There are three islands in the Shiant group which lies in the Minch, due north of Skye and due East of Harris. *Eilean an Tigh* is joined to *Eilean Murre* by a narrow, pebbly neck of land. It was at the end of this beach that Compton Mackenzie chose to build his tiny house when he owned the island and for me it is this little shelter, with the tin roof, that gives the island its human dimension and irresistible appeal. There are two rooms, with a fire place in each, and they say you can get quite comfortable whilst gazing out at the 'dragon's teeth' line of off-shore rocks and Harris beyond. This image of the lonely Hebridean dwelling appears over and over in books, paintings and postcards and has become iconic. There are gable ends, single chimney stacks, dormer style windows and red roofs in image after image, from the work of the Scottish Colourists to the modern, glazed tiles and mugs sold in airport gift shops. They tap into a primeval need in many of us to see this humanising element in an otherwise wild landscape. The house provides a reference point and a place of comfort from which to appreciate the scene.

From the house you can watch the comings and goings of the

puffins, carrying sandeels to feed their young in burrows on the island, and the human fishers dredging for scallops from the seabed in the Minch. Donald MacSween and Kenny Cunningham were two such fishermen back in 1991 when they dragged up a lump of wire in their gear. The wire was solid gold, of the purest quality and had been fashioned into a necklace or armlet some 3,000 years earlier. The Shiant island torc was late Bronze Age and it sent the Edinburgh archaeology establishment into a spin. It is about two feet long with the central section finely twisted. Each end terminates in a smooth, cylindrical piece which widens slightly towards the tip. It is a thing of stunning beauty and craftsmanship. The torc was probably intended to be worn around the neck and simply bent into place. It could, equally, be wound round as an armlet. Whoever owned it would have been someone of considerable wealth and importance. After waiting a year to see if anyone from the Bronze Age came to claim the torc (the word comes from the French torque, or twist) it was established that Donald and Kenny were the legal owners. They sold it to the National Museum of Scotland and paid off some debts. It can now be viewed in the Early People Gallery of the museum. You do have to limbo under the arm of a robot to see it, however. It seems the aim of the display's designer was to make Scotland's early treasures as difficult as possible to see. To see one gold bracelet you must climb on a bench and look at the back of a robot. I didn't know it was there until about my fifth trip to the gallery.

No one knows how the torc came to be on the sea bed off the Shiant islands. Twenty years after its discovery we are no further on than supposing it fell off a boat, was thrown off a boat as an offering or the boat sank. It is believed the torc was made circa 1200 BC when the population of Scotland was around 300,000. If the torc was thrown into the water as an offering I wonder if it was to appease the gods for the terrible conditions following the eruption of the Icelandic volcano – Hecla – around 1159 BC. About half of the population was wiped out so it was, clearly, an event of greater significance than the disruption of air travel. The Shiant torc could, however, have been lost much further south and gradually shifted northwards by prevailing currents. For three thousand years it lay in another time and in another dimension, separated from our time by a few fathoms of sea water. Donald and Kenny dragged it, as if through a spacetime wormhole, into the sunlight of the present.

I didn't make it to Shiant on this occasion. The transport arrangements wouldn't fit in the time I had available so I went to Mingulay instead. I will get there one day.

Crowded beach, Kiloran Bay, Colonsay.

Lismore lighthouse, guarding the southern entrance to the Sound of Mull.

Peaceful, *machair* campsite, Outer Hebrides.

Upper gallery view, St Magnus Cathedral, Kirkwall, Orkney.

Modern dads on Sunday morning duty, Lerwick, Shetland.

Handmade by Elizabeth Riddiford on Fair Isle, using native Shetland wool.

Pladda, from Arran.

Evening light, South Uist.

Fisher folk, Kildonan, Arran.

Islands in the Sound of Harris.

Sea arch, Mingulay.

Last flight home, South Uist.

Deserted croft, Colonsay.

Breezy day, Arran.

Evening ferry to Kirkwall from Orkney's northern isles.

Boat roof, Lerwick, Shetland.

CHAPTER 19

Flannan – A tragic mystery

EILEAN MOR IS A beautiful island. Place your hand, palm down, fingers slightly spread on the table. Now arch the palm so only fingertips and wrist remain on the surface and that is, roughly, Eilean Mor. The lighthouse is on the high point. The gaps between your fingers are steep, rocky inlets or geos. The island looks from the air a giant dinosaur claw. The awesome terror of the winter sea pounding into the geos is softened in summer by the lush green carpet of grass and flowers on the top. The white lighthouse looks a lovely place to live with the sun shining but can be obliterated at times by spray reaching 300 feet above sea level.

Historically the Flannan islands have been little more than a hazard to shipping. Also called the Seven Hunters they are seven tiny pebbles of grassy rock that add up to just over 100 acres. The biggest of the seven is Eilean Mor, which has the lighthouse and a ruin reputed to be a chapel, and Eilean Tighe, which is unspoiled. Five other islands, little more than stacks or skerries make up the group. Sitting 20 miles west of Lewis in the Outer Hebrides, they have always been too small, too remote and too inaccessible even to be used as grazing. They are classed, along with St Kilda and Rockall, as Atlantic outliers. Difficult to reach, and impossible to land on at times, these rocky specks are all the more alluring for it.

For obvious reasons it was decided to build a lighthouse on the Flannan Islands and in 1895 David Stevenson (relative of Robert Louis and the 'Lighthouse Stevenson' family) began the construction of a 75 foot tower on Eilean Mor (the big island). The island slopes up to a cliff height of 200 feet so a very tall structure wasn't needed. The light began shining in 1899 with 44-year-old James Ducat, a Principal Lightkeeper with 22 years' service, in charge. 29-year-old Thomas Marshall, Assistant Keeper, and an Occasional Keeper – Donald Macarthur were in assistance.

On 15 December 1900, the steamer *Archtor* reported in its log seeing no light on the Flannans and passed a message to the Lighthouse Board. The routine relief vessel, *Hesperus*, was already on its way to the islands and arrived on 26 December. They reported back to Edinburgh that 'A dreadful accident has happened on the Flannans.'

Landing on the island, the relief keeper, John Smith, made his way up to the light. He found the gate to the compound and the lighthouse door closed. One (of three) sets of oilskins was hanging on its peg; the kitchen was clean and tidy and the light cleaned and trimmed ready for a night of operation that never came. The beds were empty but unmade – hardly significant in a men only house. The only sign of disturbance was the half-eaten meal and a single dining chair tipped over backwards, away from the table, as though someone had leapt up in a hurry. Actually, there was no mention in the official reports of the tipped chair or the half-eaten meal. They have found their way into the legend from a poem, *Flannan Isle* written in 1912, by Wilfred William Gibson. The clock had stopped and the pet canary was starving in its cage. The lighthouse log was made up until the 15 December and nothing untoward was reported there.

Smith reported back and a visit by the superintendent followed. All sorts of fanciful explanations were put forward, from murder and suicide to capture by aliens or mythical beasts. In the end it was accepted that a freak wave must have broken over the island and washed all three men into the sea as it ebbed away. Two men may have been outside, perhaps trying to secure equipment at the landing stage during the storm, the third man could have seen the wave coming and rushed out to warn them – explaining the oilskins still on the peg.

The superintendent discounted the possibility of their having been blown off the island as the wind was in the west at that time and more likely to have blown the men up the island, rather than down to the sea. He felt they would have been able to regain their footing had there been such a gust.

James Ducat, Thomas Marshall and Donald Macarthur lost everything on that fateful day. In 1971 the Flannan lighthouse was automated and the last resident keepers taken off. Maintenance now is carried out by ship and helicopter from the National Lighthouse Board Operating Base in Oban.

All UK lighthouses are now automated, computer controlled and un-manned. The last Scottish lighthouse to have a resident crew was Fair Isle (south). It has been said that lighthouse keeping was the first profession to be made wholly redundant. In Scotland this end was reached when the Fair Isle keepers left on 31 March 1998. It was a unique way of life to which the Flannan men gave dedicated, unstinting service. It may have been their professional determination to save their employer's box of ropes from the gale that cost them their lives. They have not been forgotten in the Outer Hebrides, even now. As I write this account, a schoolteacher in Edinburgh is preparing her class to hear the story and, no doubt, they will be encouraged to speculate on what really happened.

What we do know for certain is that James Ducat left his wife, Louisa, and four children: Louisa (16), Robert (13), Anabella (9) and Arthur (6). Thomas Marshall was single and his father, John, was unsuccessful in his claim to the Lighthouse Board for compensation. Donald McArthur had served only four and a half years of the five necessary for his wife to claim a full pension. She received gratuities of £50 for herself and £20 for their two children – aged ten and seven. She could not make a living in the Outer Isles and so went back to her original home in Gravesend.

CHAPTER 20

St Kilda – Dual World Heritage Site

THERE PROBABLY NEVER was a Saint Kilda, so where do I begin to tell the story of these islands about which so much has already been written? For Scottish island aficionados a visit to this tiny archipelago is a pilgrimage but, even so, relatively few people make it out there. There is no all-weather anchorage and so those who do manage to cross the 40 miles west of Lewis might have to turn back without landing. I have visited St Kilda but, even now, it sometimes feels as though the whole thing was a hallucination.

We crossed from Skye via the Sound of Harris, in a wooden sailing boat, at night. The Atlantic swell induced wretched sea sickness in me and, as I leaned over the side being ill, I thought I saw pink dolphins. In the grey dawn I photographed Boreray, away to starboard with its own plume of mist such as you sometimes see on photographs of Everest. I had no recollection of seeing Boreray, or of taking the quite stunning photograph, even when I got my prints back from the chemist (the trip was in the summer of 1991) – but I must have been there. I did walk on St Kilda, in the sunshine, but I was so sleep-deprived and dehydrated that every time I sat down I nodded off. I was disappointed at first but then I thought people often arrive on the summit of Everest feeling not too good. I have thought of St Kilda as my personal 'Everest' since then and am reconciled. I treasure every second of the 20 hours spent ashore.

The main island of the St Kilda group is Hirte and is the only one that has been inhabited – continuously for thousands of years before its final evacuation in 1930. Islanders lived communally by growing crops, raising sheep, a little fishing and famously from collecting seabirds and their eggs in a dangerous annual harvest from the immense cliffs. The island is dotted with tiny, stone huts, called cleits, which were used for drying and storing the birds. Disease, emigration and sheer hardship caused the population to decline from almost 200 at the end of the 17th century to the 36 islanders who petitioned the government for evacuation in 1930. The increasing contact with the outside world through tourism had created a need for imported goods and, perhaps, dissatisfaction with the life that had been acceptable for so long. The last 36 souls simply did not have the physical resources for boat handling or cliff climbing. In the end there were only ten men aged between 18 and 60.

HMS *Harebell* arrived in Village Bay on the evening of 28 August 1930. Members of the press were kept away despite huge interest throughout Britain in the plight of the St Kildans. It was felt they deserved some privacy for such an emotional occasion. In the morning, a bible was left open in each house and the islanders closed their doors for good. Livestock and some furniture were taken separately. They were resettled, according to their wishes, in various parts of Scotland. Each summer, at least until the outbreak of World War II, some islanders returned to live the old life for a few months and some to act as guides for the visitors who came, like me, fascinated by their story. The houses soon fell into disrepair but have been saved by the new owners – The National Trust for Scotland (since 1957). The beautiful, curved street of abandoned houses, some restored, above the shore in Village Bay is the thing that most defines St Kilda today. Its poignancy attracts people from all over the world to gaze, over and over, at its image and to retell the story of the St Kildans.

On taking ownership of St Kilda in 1957 The National Trust for Scotland leased a plot of land below the village to the MOD who built a radar tracking station so they could tell the people at the South Uist Missile Range where their rockets were splashing down. The builders arrived – for what was known as Operation Hardrock – and quarried the Hirte hillside for stone to build the military installation. Luckily they were dissuaded by the National Trust from using stones from the houses and cleitean in Village Bay as hardcore.

Today the small base, now run by civilian contractors – QinetiQ – sits incongruously between the pier and the village street. As you walk through it, or round it, you see, hear and smell the garbage incinerator and other trappings of modern life. The ancient village beyond stands even more beguilingly and other-worldly as you approach. The base wouldn't win an architectural prize or a Visit Scotland four-star rating but its presence on St Kilda has helped to secure the island as a viable destination for researchers and visitors. QinetiQ, and MOD before them, have lived as good neighbours

with the naturalists, archaeologists, sheep researchers and histori-
ans. They have provided water, electricity, medical cover and some
transport. They have, in short, become part of the St Kilda story.

In 1986 UNESCO ascribed World Heritage Status to St Kilda in
recognition of its incomparable natural importance. There are glob-
ally significant populations of several species of seabirds, including
puffins, gannets and kittiwakes. The St Kilda mouse and St Kilda
wren are sub-species of mainland varieties and are found only on
St Kilda. They are the evolutionary products of extreme isolation
such as are more famously seen on The Galapagos Islands. In 2004
the protected area was extended to include the marine environment
surrounding St Kilda and in 2005, because of the cultural heritage
of the island, UNESCO awarded the rare Dual World Heritage Status.
There have been only twenty or so such awards and St Kilda's
recognition puts it in the same category as Uluru (Ayers Rock) in
Australia and Machu Pichu in Peru.

Today the population of Village Bay fluctuates around about 15
at the base. There's the ranger, an archaeologist, sheep researchers
and itinerant scientists looking at snails, beetles or seabirds and
such like. There was even a question raised on the internet by one
archaeologist who found a wooden stake and then another one
like it a few days later. He put a picture on the internet and asked
if anyone knew what they were. Such is the passion for St Kilda
that no stone, or stake, is left unturned in the search for answers
as to exactly how life was lived there (all stones are, very definitely,
put back where they were found of course). National Trust working parties also spend the summer carefully putting back stones
and turf that have been dislodged by winter gales. Were it not for
the ongoing conservation work the houses and cleits would have
crumbled to heaps of rubble long ago – as they have in so many of
Scotland's abandoned settlements.

The scientists lucky enough to spend a summer or two on St
Kilda will enjoy sun and blue skies. There was a two month
drought in 2008 which led to beach barbecues, swimming in the
sea and sunbathing, but also flushing toilets with sea water and
scrounging showers from visiting cruise ships. There are also days
and weeks of dreich mist, squalls, cold and more mist. The cruise
ships, provided there are not too many, are a welcome distraction
for the staff who conduct guided tours of the village area.

Throughout the summer there are seabirds to be ringed, the church to be painted, drains to be cleared, supplies to be unloaded and vigilance against rats to be kept. In 2005 a new, Gaelic bible was presented to the kirk by Fergus Macdonald of The Scottish Bible Society who felt it proper since Gaelic had been the language of the St Kildans. A remembrance service was held, attended by the few souls who were on the island at the time. Also in 2005 Norman Gillies, who had been evacuated, aged five, from St Kilda along with his family and the others in the final departure of 1930, flew in by helicopter to mark the 75th anniversary of the evacuation. Together with his new family he was photographed outside the house where he was born and had lived.

Sixty million years ago a volcano erupted from the sea bed and created St Kilda. The sea has battered it ever since, creating the caves, stacks and arches of the unique coast line we see today. The sea will,

Partially restored houses, St Kilda.

eventually, reclaim St Kilda through the process we call erosion and in a time scale we call eternity. Humans themselves may well have gone from Earth by then but, in the meantime, we keep faith with Norman Gillies and the St Kildans, and with future generations, by carefully guarding this hauntingly beautiful, fragile place.

The dolphins, by the way, were real – they were coloured pink by the navigation light on our boat. The wooden stakes dated from a 20th century electricity installation and so were not very interesting.

CHAPTER 21

Orkney Mainland – Award-winning adventures in Neolithic Orkney

IN JULY 2011 I was standing next to Nick Card, director of a stunning neolithic excavation in Orkney Mainland, when The Brodgar Boy was found. Hilary Kirk from the Wirral, a volunteer spending a week's holiday on the Ness of Brodgar dig, handed Nick a 3cm fragment of pottery. There was a 'head', a 'body' and two pin pricks where the eyes should be. A voice from the throng called out 'Behold – the Brodgar Boy,' and the name has stuck.

It is a crude piece that had clearly broken off something else in antiquity. Whoever broke it, perhaps a careless neolithic child, thought it looked like a person and added the eyes. Whatever its origin, it is a small window on the mind of an Orcadian 5,000 years ago. About a week later I learned that its 'other half' had been found. The whole was now thought to be, possibly, a human figure with legs moulded into the bottom half.

In August 2009 a similar size figure – the Westray Wife – was found in the island of Westray to the north. The Westray Wife (or Orkney Venus) and the Brodgar Boy, are two of only four neolithic, human figures found in the UK to date. The Wife had clearly been intended as a human figure from the start. The head and body are better proportioned. She has two eyes in roughly the right places and some scratches where nose and mouth should be. Two circles for breasts sit high and wide on her collar bones, but then Picasso's figures were, often, equally odd. She looks quite downcast to me – perhaps life in neolithic Orkney was as tough as I sometimes imagine.

Orkney has some of the best preserved neolithic remains in Europe and the Ness of Brodgar site is at the heart of it. The Lochs of Stenness and Harray are separated by a neck of land which narrows at its southern end. The Ring of Brodgar – a magnificent circle of standing stones has dominated this place for 5,000 years. No generation of Orcadians will have been unaware of it or failed to speculate on its significance. A mile or so to the south are the Stones of

Stenness – not quite so numerous or impressive, many having fallen in times past.

For years it has been thought these ring monuments were all there was to see on the Ness. An earthen mound in between them was believed to be just that – a naturally occurring hillock. Then in 2002 someone decided to check, and huge geophysical anomalies were indicated below the soil. Nick Card and The Orkney Research Centre for Archaeology – ORCA – arrived and started to dig.

Every summer season since then the magnificent Ness of Brodgar complex of late neolithic buildings has been gradually revealed. A massive walled enclosure was found, stretching almost across the isthmus and enclosing the buildings. There are paved walkways and roofs of slate or stone. By 2008 it was apparent this was a special place. One of the buildings (structure 10) is the largest, non-funery, stone built Neolithic structure in Britain at 25 x 20m with 5m thick walls.

In 2010 paint was detected on some wall slabs. The diversity of pottery at the Ness site indicates its use by people from all over Orkney. Some of it, for example, is very similar to that from Skara Brae – a well preserved village a few miles to the north and another of Orkney's Neolithic treasures.

The Harray and Stenness lochs, possibly just marshes in Stone Age times, lie in a natural bowl on the western side of the Orkney mainland. From anywhere on the site one can look around at the low, encircling hills and understand this could have been a very special place to people 5000 years ago.

Approaching from any direction the rings and buildings would have been impressive. 'The neolithic builders were showing off,' said Nick Card. 'This place was meant to impress, perhaps even intimidate those who came to it.'

There are sharp internal angles, beautifully coursed stone work and fine corner buttresses. It may have been a ceremonial or cult centre, a place for the consumption of special food perhaps. More than 80 separate panels have been found with finely incised, geometric art/graffiti.

The centre was almost certainly non-domestic judging by the array of Grooved Ware pottery, mace heads, axes, flint, pitchstone (volcanic glass from Arran) and animal bones found. The location, scale, symmetry and complexity all point to some kind of ritual use.

Also visible from the site is Maeshowe, a neolithic, chambered burial mound. Even without all the other structures Maeshowe would be a fabulous monument. It houses three burial alcoves built into the walls. Entry is behind a swivelling block stone, by a low, paved passage way aligned to be struck by the setting sun at the winter solstice. It has a corbelled roof which protected the interior from the elements for 4,000 years, until the Vikings broke in, probably in 1153. They came to shelter, explore and, perhaps, to plunder. In any event they left some of the finest examples of their runic inscriptions anywhere. 'Ingigerth is the most beautiful of women' and 'Thorni bedded, Helgi carved' being two such examples.

This little area of the northern isles is a window on a lost world, a puzzle for archaeologists to speculate and ruminate over for years. It is also a most wonderful place for visitors. Neolithic Orkney would give Stonehenge, Viking York and Hadrian's Wall a run for their money on any day.

The Vikings didn't confine themselves to bawdy writing, they left some other messages in Maeshowe too: 'Treasure was carried off in three nights – To the north-west is a great hidden treasure. It was long ago that treasure was hidden here.' This treasure has never been found. Professional archaeologists suggest the messages were nothing more than idle bragging – but I am not a professional archaeologist. I can choose to believe that lying somewhere under the Orcadian soil, in Quoyloo, Isbister or Skaill, is a hoard of Neolithic, Bronze Age or Viking treasure waiting to be found.

My wish for gold, silver, pottery, art, stone axes and tiny figures is not so I can be fabulously rich but so I can sit in the National Museum, in Edinburgh, and marvel at fantastic people who walked and talked in Orkney thousands of years ago. I'd love to have been a dinner guest at Ness of Brodgar, when a good fire was burning in the hearth and there was fresh fish on the menu.

In 1958, aged 15, Douglas Coutts found a boxful of 8th century silver concealed below a ruined chapel on St Ninian's Isle, Shetland. Douglas heard about the dig at a lecture his father had taken him to. He volunteered to help and, although the excavations had been ongoing for three years, found the collection after just three hours on his first day. The St Ninian Hoard is one of Scotland's greatest treasures and is now on permanent display in the National Museum. After its discovery the find was spirited away to London overnight and Douglas didn't see it again until the following year when it returned, briefly, to Shetland having been cleaned and conserved. Some years later he was one of the volunteers keeping vigil when the hoard was once again on loan to Shetland.

Round the corner in the museum are the Lewis chessmen. Only 11 of the 93 pieces remain in Scotland, the rest having been sold to the British Museum shortly after their discovery in 1831. The medieval, ivory gaming pieces, of Scandinavian origin, are among the most famous of Scotland's ancient treasures but no one really knows how they got to Lewis. They are loaned out for exhibition round the world from time to time, including Museum nan Eilean in Stornoway.

I call to look at these fabulous, untouchable and unknowable links to Scotland's past every time I'm in Edinburgh. I'd love to speak to the folk who made and used them.

I did speak to Douglas recently. He's coming up to a big birthday this year and still loves to talk about the St Ninian silver. He would prefer it had a permanent home in Shetland but I think such things are best kept in Edinburgh, where everyone can see them. School children and others, travel to Edinburgh from all over Scotland. In a single visit to the museum they can see so many wonderful things that have been collected from places that would be very difficult – and expensive – to visit individually. One nation, after all.

I visited Ness of Brodgar, again, in 2013. It is now thought the 'Brodgar Boy' may not be a human figure after all. It is being called by the diggers, rather disrespectfully, 'the Brodgar Jobby'.

Should you discover the Maeshowe Viking treasure anytime soon then you will not have far to go to get it properly excavated. If you can find them, then maybe you can hire... The O Team.

The dig at Ness of Brodgar is being carried out by ORCA[1] (The Orkney Research Centre for Archaeology) for local interested parties[2] but if you have a building development project – anything from a single house plot to a commercial development – requiring professional archaeological investigation before it can continue then ORCA will be glad to oblige.

Notes

1 ORCA – Orkney Research Centre for Archaeology is part of The
Orkney College, itself a member of UHI – University of Highlands and
Islands. ORCA has its own geophysics unit. To find out more about
Ness of Brodgar there is a daily, online dig diary at: www.orkneyjar.
com or you can visit ORCA at www.orca.uhi.ac.uk Nick Card is avail-
able to discuss ways in which ORCA might help with your project.
Nick.Card@uhi.ac.uk Tel: 01856569342 Fax: 01856569017

2 The excavations are supported by Orkney Islands Council, Orkney
College UHI, the Russel Trust, the Robert Kiln Trust, Orkney Archaeology Society, Orkneyjar.com, Historic Scotland, numerous individuals
from around the world and the landowners Carol Hoey and Ola and
Arnie Tait.

Nick Card with archaeological find, Orkney.

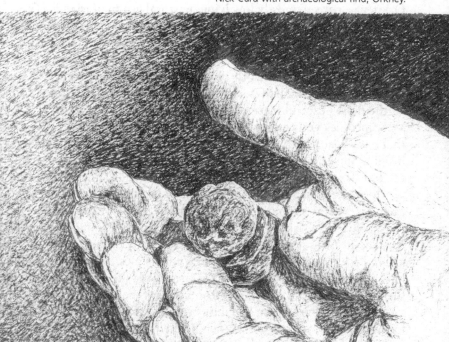

CHAPTER 22

Orkney – Carving the runes

THE ORKNEY ISLANDS are in the north. On a clear day South Ronald-say and Hoy can be seen from John O'Groats. Their most famous sons are probably: the Old Man of Hoy – a rock stack, and St Magnus – a saint, murdered by his cousin in 1117 and in whose honour a beautiful red sandstone cathedral stands in the centre of Kirkwall.

Orcadians pursue the usual island industries of farming fishing and tourism. It is said that what distinguishes them from their neighbours in Shetland, to the farther north, is that Shetlanders are fishermen with crofts whereas Orcadians are crofters with boats. Orkney is a green, mostly low lying, pastoral group of islands. The people are some of the most welcoming and friendly anywhere and, when the sun shines, the vistas are alternate bands of green grass, blue sea, white clouds and blue sky. From any slight bit of vantage the colours in the patchwork of fields and wild flowers are fabulous. In April 2013, analysis of crime statistics revealed Orkney to be the most peaceful place in Scotland to live.

Sometimes you cannot improve on the description of an island that has already been made, often by a local with a deep and loving insight. Sometimes you have to tell the stories of the locals to get the full flavour of the place and, so, in this account I have tried to see things as local author George Mackay Brown saw and reported them, as well as adding a few observations of my own.

When I first visited Orkney, in 1988, I read a few of George Mackay Brown's novels and short stories – many of them set in and around the history of Orkney from Viking times. More recently I have discovered his modern short essays, about life as viewed from the bench seat on the pier in Stromness, or the bus to Kirkwall. George was a lovely man, loved by everyone that knew him before his death, aged 75, in 1996. When he died a sculptor, an outsider, tried to sell the town the idea of a bust of George 'for fear he is forgotten' but Tam McPhail at the bookshop told me 'That was an absurd idea, the man clearly did not understand Stromness. People do not die here, it is just as if they have gone into the next room. George will never be forgotten.'

George Mackay Brown lived and worked his entire life in Stromness. He was an Orcadian, a Stromnessian, man and boy. The Booker Prize nominated 'Bard of Orkney' could have travelled the world but, apart from Edinburgh University and a travelling scholarship to Dublin, he hardly ever left home – he never visited England, apart from crossing the river, briefly, at Berwick and a trip to Oxford.

Born in 1921 he was 38 before *Loaves and Fishes*, his first collection of poems, was published and 51 before the first novel, *Greenvoe*, appeared. GMB was happiest when he was writing, describing the periods of depression between his productive times as 'the desert.' His time at Edinburgh University and the publications of his work had been 'oases.' He was afflicted by tuberculosis in his teens and, in the days before powerful antibiotics, he felt he had been condemned to an unproductive life. George would, however, refer to 'his friend the tubercle' who kept him free from the treadmill of 'getting and spending' and allowed him to indulge his intellectual, and more particularly, his literary pursuits.

For what would be almost the last 25 years of his life he wrote a weekly column for the local newspaper, *The Orcadian*. He wrote about the most absurdly mundane, the poetic, the everyday and the poignant moments of his life and the lives of fellow Stromnessians. He wrote of picnics, Vikings, street-lighting and the Dounby show. He described his way of working (always in biro at the kitchen table – 9am until noon each day) and the things he saw during a bus ride to Kirkwall. He describes the demise of his electric toaster, the kindness of friends, eating kippers and feeding next door's cat. He glories in Rockpools and Daffodils (the title of his last collection of letters). He talks of walking into town to collect 'messages' which I now understand to be items of shopping.

In spite of bouts of depression which dogged him all his life ('In sooth, I know not why I am so sad/It wearies me.') and the flare-ups of the TB, George Mackay Brown paints a picture of a contented, sufficient-unto-the-day kind of life that we competitors in the rat race always imagine to be there for the taking in the islands. I rented a fisherman's cottage by the pier in George's Stromness, and went to see if I could taste the kippers.

Stromness is delightful. One has the feeling of having travelled much further abroad. You could just as easily be in a Norwegian fishing village if it were not for the signs saying: 'Julia's Café', 'Bookshop' or 'Pier Arts Centre'. The memory that most visitors will take away from Stromness is the ribbon of flagstones forming the main street along the full length of the town, which at little more than 1km is an easy stroll.

Fishermen's houses and cottages huddle on the steep side of the hill – Brinkie's Brae – on the west side of the street and another, single row of cottages backs onto the water's edge on the east side. Each waterfront dwelling has its own stone pier and slipway which were originally built by the merchant occupiers for trading directly with whatever vessels might be in the harbour.

The cottages are separated by narrow closes giving access to the shore on one side, or more houses on the other. The closes would be called gennells, snickets or entries in other parts of the world. The closes lead up, or down, invitingly from the street and a full afternoon can be enjoyed exploring up one, along a bit, and then down the next to return to the street. Often these alleys, some of which are blind, are no more than one flagstone wide, and you get the uncomfortable feeling that you are walking up someone's garden path. Usually however the effort will give access to another flight of stone steps, a turning onto a lane and yet another vista of the harbour, the step-gabled roofs, gardens or church spire that give Stromness such a unique character.

Stromness has an Arctic feel to it. Not because it is cold, although it is a few degrees below an average day in Torquay, but because of all the associations it has. There is Franklin Road, named after Sir John Franklin who sailed from here in the 1840s in search of the north-west passage. There is Rae's Close, now a sheltered housing scheme, remembering Dr John Rae, an Orkneyman who worked for the Hudson Bay Company and who sailed after Franklin in 1853, discovering both the fate of Franklin and, ironically, the north west passage.

Login's Well, outside the former Login's Hotel, is a curiosity in the main street. Franklin, Rae, Captain Cook and whaling captains all drew fresh water here before catching the tide, westwards through Hoy Sound. They won't have sailed before a dram at Login's, run by Margaret Login, an agent of the Hudson Bay Company, and certainly not before walking up Brinkie's Brae, the hill that watches over the town, to buy a fair wind from Bessie Millie for sixpence.

Stromness is not a resort. The picturesque waterfront of stone piers and cottages does not have a promenade along which one might enjoy the sea view or the facades. To take in the whole scene the visitor must climb the hill or cross the harbour and look back from the ferry pier. During my exploration, each time I passed the end of a close I wandered down to stand on a little pier or boat slip and look into the clear Orkney water (Shellfish from here are highly prized for having grown pollution free). In the 1980s, at the time of my first visit, a campaign was being run under the banner 'Keep Orkney Green and Active, not White and Radioactive.' Some folk wanted to mine for Uranium in the islands.

George Mackay Brown delighted in his Stromness childhood to which there are many references in his weekly letters to the *The Orcadian.*[1] One of his favourite haunts was Clouston's Pier 'because all my earliest memories are of it (the fishermen baiting their lines, the old woman swilling headless haddocks, the boys bathing in the summer)'. With his pals he would catch sillocks and sell them to 'wives with cats' at four for a penny.

Lest we think all that innocence gone for good, I met a group of Stromness lads idling away a Sunday afternoon on the pier. 'Do you fish?' I asked. 'Yes, we catch sillocks and give them to the cats.' I asked what they knew of Mackay Brown and between them they managed that he wrote poetry books, was born in 1921 and had blue eyes. They found amusing my suggestion that they should sell their catches for the index linked equivalent of four for a penny. Perhaps they have things too easy in Orkney as elsewhere. They were very personable lads for all that and we chatted amiably for ten minutes or so. 'We like living in Orkney,' the leader said. 'Because it is safe and we are free.'

George Mackay Brown was a great observer and reporter of the mundane. He found pleasure in so many things and was able to draw inspiration and interest from them for his columns in *The Orcadian*. One day in April 1971 he caught the bus from Stromness to Kirkwall. In April 2005 I did the same thing so we could compare notes. It only cost George 'five bob return' a price he considered 'good value compared to the three and six it had cost in pre-war days.' My return fare was £3.30 which, I suppose, was even better. We passed a swimming pool and fitness centre on our way out of town which George would have marvelled at, no doubt comparing it with bathing from Clouston's Pier. The rain over the Hoy hills was pretty much as it had been, and the butter-cups and king cups in the water-logged field fringes were no differ-ent. Many of the ewes had twin lambs and the wind was whipping up 'white horses' on Stenness and Harray Lochs. The neolithic Ring of Brodgar standing stones, and the fantastic Maeshowe bur-ial chamber were most certainly unchanged.

The Orkney poet will have been familiar with the potter work-ing in Harray for the tourist market, but would not appreciate his more recent advertising slogan in which he claims to be: 'The Original Harray Potter' The first view of St Magnus Cathedral as the bus neared Kirkwall has not changed and, in short, I suppose, the landscape of Orkney is proving to be fairly timeless.

There are some more obvious impacts of progress on the envi-ronment: the wind turbines have arrived in the last 15 years or so and the noise from the generators on MV *Hamnavoe*, the new ferry on the Scrabster run, hums over the whole town when she is lying alongside the pier.

I do wish we could get to grips with noise pollution. It seems an absurdity to me that I can travel to one of the most beautiful, tran-quil, historic little towns in Europe, be surrounded by sea and sky, wild flowers and birds and yet be unable to use the front bedroom of my holiday cottage because of generator noise all night.[2]

There are speed bumps on some of the new housing develop-ments above the town and one or two of the young lads have the standard issue Golf GTis, the ones with the base speakers filling the boot. Even in St Magnus Cathedral the phone was ringing when I walked in on my last morning.

George Mackay Brown is buried in Warbeth Cemetary, facing the sea just outside Stromness. I was having some difficulty finding his marker in the sprawling plot so I asked an old lady tending a grave if she knew where it was. 'Morag,' she called over a wall 'Do you know where George is buried?' She clearly felt no need to mention the surname. Between them they soon found the grave and I was able to pay my respects.

'Carve the runes then be content with silence' it said. This was a line taken from one of George's last poems: 'A Work for Poets'.

Much of George's writing had been a search for silence. Not the kind of silence I have been ranting about but the silence that comes from having said, or written, something so perfectly that there is no need for further comment.

Notes

1 Collections of George's letters have been published in several volumes which make delightful bedtime reading: See Further Reading
2 Since this visit I heard that *MV Hamnavoe* has a new, quieter generator.
3 I visited again in 2013 – it isn't any quieter.

CHAPTER 23

Orkney – The energy islands

SOMETHING VERY SPECIAL is happening in the Orkney Islands. If you think of the California gold rush and the North Sea oil bonanza you may not be far wide of the mark. Quite simply the Orkney Islands have become the world capital for research and development of wave and tidal energy.

Nowhere else on Earth has as much commitment to harnessing wave and tidal energy for the generation of electricity as does Orkney. Of 18 experimental installations currently operating in the world, eight are in Orkney's waters. Orkney cut her teeth on renewable energy exploitation in the '70s with the installation on Burgar Hill of the, then, largest wind turbine in the world.

The islands have a unique set of qualities that lend themselves well to carrying out the work needed. Firstly they have both strong tides *and* exposure to plenty of energetic waves. The tides are forced through a collection of inter-island races providing good locations for both fixed and moveable, tidally operated generators. In addition the waves created by the prevailing, south-westerly Atlantic winds are constant and considerable.

Orkney also has the infrastructure to exploit this green energy. There are communities close at hand, in the towns of Stromness and Kirkwall, home to many of Orkney's 20,000 people. There is a strong maritime tradition, from the days of whaling and exploration. Fishing is still an important activity here. The people know and respect the seas around Orkney and are ideally suited to the work needed.

Furthermore there is an advanced skills base in the islands which is supported by the Orkney College – part of the University of the Highlands and Islands. Intellectual capital was much developed in Orkney by the arrival of the Flotta Oil terminal in the 1970s. The population of the islands could well have fallen to 15,000, or fewer, at that time had not the oil arrived to boost employment and the local economy.

Finally, in the list of Orcadian advantages, is its proximity to a ready market place for electricity – the Scottish mainland. Orkney could generate 20,000 GWh of electricity annually from renewable sources, more than the entire Scottish government target for such power by 2020. One limiting factor on this development at present is the capacity of the two submarine cables to carry electricity from Orkney to Scotland. As generating capacity increases further new cables will be needed but this is not seen as a problem. The question to be sorted out, as ever, is who will pay for them?

Marine renewable energy is still a relatively young industry, with plenty of brave, young men and women accepting the risks and challenges necessary to develop the commercial possibilities. Gareth Davies, managing director of Aquatera – one of numerous companies operating in Orkney, has brought together other companies to form Orkney Marine Renewable Support (OMRS).

As more and more enterprises seek permission to use Orkney's sea as a test bed for their equipment OMRS offers a locally based, and highly knowledgeable, group of people who can offer advice. People seeking to test equipment need to know, precisely, about wave and tidal conditions. They need to know the relative strength of tides from week to week. They need information on seabed conditions, for example, and the likely effects of their work on wildlife in any given season. All these surveys are required by government before test licenses are granted. People based locally are well equipped to help and advise. Aquatera is also developing a worldwide portfolio of customers seeking similar advice.

Orkney has established a permanent, shore-based marine renewable base for client companies to use. The new chairman of Orkney Renewable Energy Forum (OREF) Pete Tipler is very proud of the work being undertaken in what he calls The Energy Islands. So proud are they all, in fact, that Neil Kermode, Stevie Burns and Richard Gauld have collaborated to launch a website which offers live reports of Orkney's instantaneous energy production from renewable sources.

The site compares output from renewables with the archipelago's current demand for electricity. Writing this on a dreich Thursday morning in October I have just paused to check the site. Orkney is demanding 20.62MW of electricity from the grid of which 11.70MW are being supplied by renewable sources. At other times they have generated 100 per cent of demand from renewables.[1]

Locally based company – Scotrenewables Tidal Power Ltd – has recently connected their prototype tidal turbine to the grid. The SR250 is anchored in the water at the European Marine Energy Centre (EMEC) tidal test site at Billia Croo off Orkney Mainland's west coast.

Also in the water is *Pelamis* – a huge, hinged metal snake that generates electricity as the waves beneath it cause it to flex as it rises and falls. There is also the *Penguin* – a 500kw device that generates electricity as it rolls, heaves and pitches with each passing wave. *Oyster* 2, another wave powered device, began trials in 2011. It is hard to imagine the scale of these things from descriptions but when I was parked in the ferry queue at Kirkwall recently I found myself next to the biggest propeller I had ever seen, casually waiting to be anchored in a tide race somewhere.

These are exciting times in the northern lands. Orkney can establish itself as the world leader in marine energy research, development and supply. In this industry, however, the work will be clean and quiet. There will be no need to worry about factory effluent, noise pollution or spoiling the environment. Orkney already has a reputation for clean air and beautiful, unspoilt surroundings. The harnessing of wave and tidal power should sit very comfortably here.

Of course we cannot clog all the Orkney seaways with limitless floating gadgets, anchored to the seabed. Potential hazards to navigation will need to be minimised, effects on wildlife considered and the view from the cliff tops must be preserved.

I am not as concerned as I would be, however, if we were talking about oil, coal or nuclear powered power stations to be built in Orkney's green and pleasant land. Here is a development we can look forward to greedily. There might be a time when we can indulge ourselves with hot tubs, electric cars, heated homes and greenhouses without having to feel guilty about the environment. It is not, generally, the consumption of electricity that damages the environment but the generation of it.

The school students in Stromness Academy and Kirkwall Grammar School today need not plan to leave Orkney to find work and excitement. Orkney is one of the most forward looking, dynamic communities in Britain – the world even. Young Orcadians can anticipate a period of prosperity and ecologically sound, limitless development and yet still expect to play in green fields and walk by some of the most stunningly beautiful, unspoiled scenery.

The Neolithic farmers that built the first Orkney left a legacy of architecture, unrivalled anywhere on Earth. They knew and appreciated what they had. The modern builders and installers of 'wet metal' are doing the same.

Note

1 You can check how much renewable energy Orkney is producing, minute by minute, at www.oref.co.uk

CHAPTER 24

Egilsay – The murder of a Saint

TOWARDS THE END Orkney was handed over to Sigurd the Power-ful by the king of Norway. Sigurd, thus, became the first Earl of Orkney. Over the next 300 years or so the title passed through the hands of, among others, Turf-Einar, Thorfinn Skull-Splitter, Hlodvir, Sigurd the Stout, Sumarlidi, Einar Wry-Mouth and another Thorfinn. I mention these names for no other reason than that I like the look, and sound, of them.

The seeds of trouble were sown when the Earldom was split, on Thorfinn's death, between his two sons: Paul and Erlend. Thorfinn died in 1064 so we, non-historians, have a convenient time-refer-ence point for the action – the Battle of Hastings and the Norman conquest. Paul and Erland coped OK but problems started with *their* two sons: the cousins Haakon and Magnus. Haakon and Magnus were set against each other by the poisonous whisperings of trouble makers, particularly in Haakon's camp. When matters eventually came to a head they arranged a peace conference on the island of Egilsay.

Haakon and Magnus agreed to travel separately to Egilsay, each with a retinue of just two ships and equal numbers of men. Magnus arrived first on the tiny island and soon saw Haakon on the way – with *eight* ships. Clearly there was treachery afoot. The pious and peace-loving Magnus refused to run, yet forbade his fol-lowers from risking their own lives by fighting to protect him. 'Things must go according to God's will,' he told them.

Magnus spent the night praying in the small church and went out to face Haakon in the morning. So concerned was Magnus for his cousin's soul that he feared Haakon would be damned if he were to kill an innocent man.

'To save you from violating your oaths I will make three offers and you may take your pick,' said Magnus. 'First, I could go on pil-grimage to Rome and never return to Orkney or, second, you could exile me to Scotland.' These two options were quickly rejected so Magnus upped the ante: 'You can mutilate me or blind me and lock me in a dungeon.' When I first read this final offer of Magnus's I thought I would rather be killed than suffer mutilation and incarceration. Magnus, however, was thinking of Haakon's immortal soul and he figured this would protect the cousin from his own villainy. Haakon must have had a softer side to his nature as he was prepared to accept the mutilation offer. His men were not. They insisted things must be fixed once and for all so there could never be joint rule again. One of the leaders must die. Haakon chose Magnus for the chop.

Haakon had some difficulty in finding a willing executioner however and, in the end, ordered Lifolf, his cook, to wield the axe. Magnus comforted the poor chap and told him not to feel guilty. Magnus prayed, stood in front of Lifolf and said 'Strike me hard on the head, it's not fitting for a chieftain to be beheaded like a thief'. He then stooped to receive the blow.

Egilsay is an island of just 650 hectares and fewer than 50 people live there today. It is a low lying speck close to Rousay and Wyre and given over to farming. The school was mothballed in 2004 and finally closed in 2011. Any young families that moved to Egilsay now would have to send their children to Rousay for their primary education and then further afield – to Kirkwall or Stromness – to continue their studies.

Prominent on the hill, as the ferry approaches the pier at Skaill, is the beautiful, round tower of St Magnus church. The small building is derelict but you can still wander through the nave and appreciate the stillness. It would be lovely to stand and imagine Magnus spending the night in prayer here but, sadly, this is not that church, although it probably stands on the same site. The scene of the murder is not far off and is marked by a stone plinth.

Orkneyinga Saga reports that Haakon felt some remorse for the death of his cousin. He even attended a feast that Thora, Magnus's mother, had prepared for them both, to celebrate what she had hoped would be a successful meeting. Thora begged Haakon to be merciful and give her Magnus's body that she may bury it decently. Haakon had had a few pints by this point and was moved to tears. 'Bury your son wherever you wish,' he said.

Earl Magnus was carried to Birsay, in the north west of Orkney Mainland, and buried in Christ's Church. Haakon went on a long pilgrimage to Rome and Jerusalem, returning to Orkney to become a fine administrator and firm but fair ruler.

Following the death of plain Earl Magnus a number of claims

had been made of miraculous cures being associated with his grave at Birsay. The Bishop of Orkney declared him Saint Magnus, and made 16 April, the day of his death, St Magnus Day.

In 1129 Haakon's son, Paul, was overthrown by Magnus's nephew, who became Earl Rognvald (taking the name of a previous earl). In 1137 Earl Rognvald began the building of St Magnus Cathedral in Kirkwall and had the saint's remains brought there to their final resting place.

St Magnus Cathedral stands in Kirkwall's main shopping street between the bookshop and a small cafe that used to be the tourist information office. Across the road is an electrical goods store and a shop selling cuddly puffins to the tourists. It is as modest a location for such a magnificent building as one could possibly find.

The cathedral was built using a mixture of local, red and yellow sandstone which create a beautifully soft, warm colour effect both inside and out. It is an imposing building, especially when seen from a good vantage. The street door however, at the west end of the nave, is only a little above head height and gives the cathedral a very human dimension as you enter.

Once inside, the visitor is immersed in fabulous colour on all sides. The immense pillars, arches and vaults look as if they could withstand any force and yet provide a surprisingly intimate home for some of Orkney's treasures and treasured memories.

St Magnus in Kirkwall is the only fully medieval cathedral in Scotland. Building started in 1137 and by the end of the 12th century the nave, choir, north and south transepts had been built. During the 13th century St Rognvald's Chapel was added and in the 15th century the nave was extended westwards. Toilets have been added in the modern era.

St Magnus Cathedral has taken 875 years to build to its present form. Even today bits and pieces of art are being added. English masons from Durham cathedral laid some of the first stones but none of them saw the finished cathedral. Later builders, too, may have spent their entire working lives on the site, only to see small advances. A full working life of (say) 40 years is only five per cent of the life of the cathedral so far. Each one of those workers may have felt their contribution insignificant but there have only been 20 or so, consecutive periods of 40 years in the building's entire life. The very fact that we can date the additions to certain centuries stems, in part, from identifying the differing styles and techniques used in the architecture and construction.

My father was a carpenter and when asked by the local vicar to repair some woodwork in the church said that he could do the job but the style would not match the old fittings exactly. The vicar said that would be fine. 'The church should be a history of all the craftsmen who worked on it during its lifetime,' he said. 'Please be sure to carve your name and the date into what you do.'

Apart from the stone work forming the shell and most obvious character of the cathedral there are many, tiny features that have been added over the years and, as the vicar said: 'become the history of the people'.

Interred in one of the pillars are the bones of St Magnus himself. They were discovered when a loose block was removed for repointing, during restoration work in 1919. In the days before DNA and radiocarbon technology their identification rested on the apparent axe cut to the skull caused when Magnus was slain.

In the choir is a memorial to the 833 men of HMS *Royal Oak*, torpedoed in nearby Scapa Flow in 1939 (I learned in 2013 that recent research now puts the figure at 834). An enemy submarine escaped detection to enter the Flow and sink the battleship as she lay at anchor. The ship's bell, recovered from the seabed, is fixed here.

In a far corner of the cathedral, in St Rognvald's Chapel, just below the east window, is a collection of small plaques commemorating some of Orkney's distinguished and much loved twentieth century writers, such as Edwin Muir and George Mackay Brown.

In 1980 Maureen Farquarson, a school art teacher from the Isle of Arran, wanted to bring a party of 14 year old school students to the St Magnus Arts Festival, held every year since 1975, in Orkney. Maureen felt that to come bearing gifts would be appropriate and so decided on a piece of art work that the students could execute and take to Orkney, as an act of friendship and to form a link between the two island communities.

The result of Maureen's project can be seen today, on display in St Rognvald's Chapel. The students worked in their lunchtimes and Saturdays to produce 14 beautiful mural panels, in acrylic and gold leaf, each one depicting a chapter in the saga of St Magnus. The panels are in the tradition of medieval narrative painting – showing two scenes in each panel.

Hazel Currie was one of the Arran children who worked on the murals and when I tracked her down – she is a professional artist on Arran today – she remembered the school trip to Orkney very well. 'We were thrilled by the fact that they had a branch of Boots in Kirkwall – we don't have one on Arran,' she said.

St Rognvald's Chapel has a font inlaid with stones brought by the children of Orkney from every parish and island to mark the 850th anniversary of the cathedral in 1987. In the same year Her Majesty Queen Elizabeth II made the trip north to unveil a commemorative window above the west door and help celebrate the 850th anniversary.

When I look at the stones in the font, the Arran murals and the ship's bell they seem very tiny and insignificant against the massive stones yet they represent a couple of generations in the life of the cathedral. A few hundred years from now people will look at these things and they will have faded into the historic fabric, just as the carved grave slabs appear to us today. Faded but still there.

The children's stones, the bones, plaques, murals and grave slabs will remain in the cathedral for as long it stands. All the small, personal contributions have added up to 875 years so far and there will be more in the next millennium all being well.

Earl Rognvald and a few of his successors, the men who commissioned the building, had a vision of what it would be like and why they were building it but I wonder if the masons and labourers did. In successive centuries, as they toiled to add the latest phase of construction, did they wonder much about the contributions they were making to something significant and lasting, or were they more concerned with wages to put bread and meat on the table for their families, health and safety or, perhaps, having to work high on the scaffold during an Orkney winter? They were on a public building project after all and must have worried about how long the funding would last, just as workers do today.

There is a feeling, an atmosphere in St Magnus Cathedral, just as there is in the abbey on Iona and places like it. It makes the visitor pause to reflect, to feel the weight of history pressing down and stretching back into the mists of time. It gives us a permanent reminder of who we are and where we have come from. The cathedral shows us what successive generations have considered important.

Archaeologists in Orkney believe that, perhaps, we should not consider Ring of Brodgar and other such monuments as having been built to a plan, where the end result was the aim. The social and community effort required for the building – over a long period of time – was the important thing. Maybe we should view the cathedral in the same light.

CHAPTER 25

South Ronaldsay – 5,000 years of crab fishing

ALAN AND JOYCE CRAIGIE'S restaurant, The Creel, has an unimposing frontage, overlooking the bay at St Margaret's Hope in the south of Orkney Mainland. It is an old fisherman's house, built end-on to the sea and with a traditional, crow-stepped gable. Even driving through the village you could easily miss it and a visitor to Orkney's capital, Kirkwall, would certainly not dine here unless they knew something already. The dining room walls are hung with quality, sea-themed art and the sunsets over the bay from the window could be a cliché were they not so lovely.

Alan, the chef, has had an entry in the Good Food Guide every year since 1993 and, in 2011, achieved 37th place in the coveted top 50. The Creel is a small eaterie at just 30 covers. He does not open at lunchtimes, preferring to concentrate on offering a fine dining experience in the evening. The Creel closes in the dead of winter for Alan and Joyce to indulge their other passion – eating at the best places in Edinburgh, London and Europe, and they admit to eating a big slice of The Creel's profits.

Although not a specialist seafood restaurant, there is always local fish or shellfish on the menu alongside slow-cooked, seaweed reared North Ronaldsay lamb. The breakfast menu (The Creel is a restaurant with rooms) offers kippers smoked over shavings from an Orkney chairmaker. But it was Orkney crab, in particular, I had come to talk to Alan about. The crab starter at the Creel is a must try. A cone of white meat on a thinner base of the brown is served with apple mayonnaise and marinated cucumber. Alan places crab at the very top of the shellfish league and says the secret is to get the blend of white and brown meat just right. The richer flavoured brown must not dominate.

Much depends on the season, where the crabs have been feeding and the handling and processing of course. Deep water crabs have watery meat so the largely in-shore Orkney crab fishers catch the best crabs. Alan makes the short drive to Lamb Holm twice a week to hand pick crabs from the boat as they are landed. Food yards, not food miles.

Orkney crab has a long history of sustainability. Mesolithic hunter-gatherers threw crab and lobster remains onto their middens 5,000 years ago for Orcadian archaeologists to enthuse about when they uncovered the magnificent Stone Age dwellings at Skara Brae in Orkney's West Mainland. It is likely that crab has been on the menu in these northern islands ever since.

Until the 1970s, however, crab was not considered the delicacy it is today. Lobster was the crustacean of choice and crofters could make a very good additional income 'going to the creels' in a small boat after a day in the fields. Like so many fisheries, however, the lobster has been over-exploited by bigger boats and higher technology. Crofters needed to set more and more creels to catch fewer and fewer lobsters.

Brown crabs (known locally as partans) were plentiful but largely ignored until the 1970s. Creelers would occasionally bring them home to give to neighbours, people without a boat or those no longer able to go to sea. This free sharing of the ocean bounty is a vestige of communal living that had sustained island folk since Skara Brae was thriving.

In recent years crab has been sought out by 'foodie' consumers and promoted by supermarkets as a healthy option. The Orkney Fishermen's Society (OFS), formed in 1953 to protect the lobster fishery, now devotes huge resources to crab conservation and development. White crab meat can fetch around £49/kilo with the brown meat selling for £9.50/kilo, largely for the production of crab pate.

The philosophy of not wasting a scrap of material from a hunted animal – that was a corner stone of early societies – is embraced by Orkney crab processors who might send on the cleaned shells for use as fancy serving receptacles, or to China where the chitin is extracted for perfume manufacture, carpet dyes, pharmaceuticals and battlefield dressings.

One great benefit that derives from the Orkney crabbers owning the OFS cooperative is that they can operate quality control at the point of capture. They know what the customers need. Size selection, for conservation, is also operated right there in the boat. EU rules demand no crab smaller than 140 mm is used but OFS boats

do not land female crabs less than 153mm across. This allows
another breeding season which, at half a million eggs a year, offers
a lot of potential new crabs.

Discerning shoppers value the provenance of Orkney crab. Marks
and Spencer, who stock 11 Orkney crab products, include a picture
on the packet and name of the boat from which the meat was landed.
The chain of custody of that crab can be followed from sea bed to
supermarket freezer cabinet.

It is a very tough life for a fisherman. The seas around Orkney
are among the most challenging anywhere in the world. Small boats,
with men often working alone, navigate waves and tide rips to harvest the very best quality crabs. They combine these ancient skills
with 21st century processing, hygiene and rapidly bringing to market
consistently high quality food. Think about the men of the *Boy
James* and the *Samantha Jane* next time you tuck in to a crab on
toast starter at a posh dinner.

In a final twist to this tale of Orkney's green credential it is
worth noting that the islands are also at the forefront of research
into wave and tidal energy. Orkney is one of the few places in the
UK to have both strong tides and energetic waves. We should be
careful not to go overboard with our rush to be green, however.
There is some suggestion that the wave installations may interfere
with the crab and lobster grounds. Orkney Fishermen's Society has
appointed Sarah Lamb, a marine scientist, to investigate. Sarah is
tagging and releasing crabs at the beautifully named Billia Croo off
the west coast of Mainland Orkney. One has turned up, over 100
miles away, in the Outer Hebrides, although it is not known whether
it walked sideways all the way.

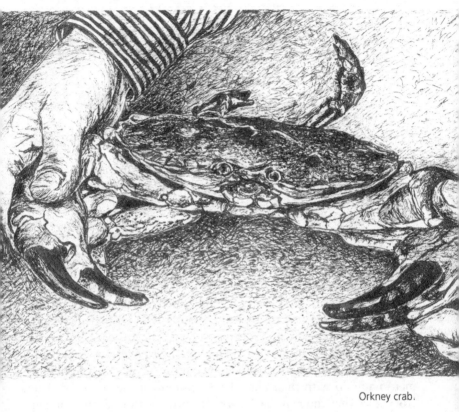

Orkney crab.

CHAPTER 26

Orkney – A lovely place to spend a wet day

THERE ARE AROUND 30 Orkney Islands and they can be viewed in a variety of ways. You can visit as an archaeologist, birdwatcher, historian or renewable energy boffin. You can just go for peace, quiet and Orcadian hospitality if you like. I've done most of these visits but in June of 2011 I went to look at the Orkney Craft Association Trail.

Every tourist destination has a souvenir market and, no matter how intellectual one might be about archaeology or history, visitors love to take away a souvenir. Jewellery, pottery and pictures are often lumped together as 'crafts'.

Tradition has it that Orkney furniture used to be made from driftwood, there being few trees on the islands. The Orkney chair has a wooden frame and seat but is backed with the more readily available straw and the local museum has examples over 100 years old.

Women's chairs had a straw cowl continuation of the back and men made do with their chair back stopping at head height. The story goes that the high backs were to protect from drafts coming through the croft house door. Robert Towers, who made my chair for me, said he thought that was a fanciful notion and people just made whatever they had the time, materials and inclination for. Mine is the basic model, without cowl or under-seat drawer.

Further along the trail, at Fursbreck Pottery in Harray, is Andrew Appleby, the self-styled 'Harray Potter'. Typical of many local craft artists Andrew is a one man band and, of course, you can watch him at work.

Pottery fragments are among some of the earliest artefacts found at pre-historic human habitations. They have had a great significance for people since they were first made and they seem to be deeply embedded in our psyche. They would have been strictly utilitarian at first but early humans quickly learned to decorate them. Many people today have vases, jugs, and plates as nothing more than decorative items in display cabinets. In early human society something that contains a liquid conveniently would have been treasured, and we have treasured them ever since.

At Fursbreck Pottery Andrew is investigating neolithic pottery from Skara Brae, Ness of Brodgar and Tomb of the Eagles – three of Orkney's pre-historic sites. He is examining how they were made and working on re-creating them. His 'Ancient Narrative' range is a development from this work. Andrew gave me a 'Bronze Age' cup he had made and it is one of the most thought-provoking things I have.

Later, I stood outside The Woolshed with owner, Denise Dupres, on the north east coast road, opposite the island of Rousay. The sun was bright and the classic Orcadian scene of alternating colour bands was fantastic.

I was trying to resist buying a North Ronaldsay wool blanket Denise had made. Farmers on North Ronaldsay build their walls to keep sheep *off* the pasture. The grass is so valuable to them for other uses that the sheep have had to content themselves with seaweed from the shore for generations. They seem to thrive on it nevertheless and produce lovely wool and meat. The ewes are allowed on the grass around lambing time however.

So, how could I possibly justify buying a woollen blanket? Too small for a double bed, not cheap and my car was already full. It is a thing of beauty however and so I bought it. It is an emotional link to the island for me when I am at home. I use it as a throw on my reading chair and it is with me now, with my Orkney chair, ceramic mugs from countless islands and my tapestry print from Hoxa.

Hoxa is way down on South Ronaldsay – where Leila Thomson, has her weaving workshop. Leila belongs to a large, artistic family. Sister Sheila has a jewellery business (Sheila Fleet) in which she is supported by sister Dorothy – trained in art and glass work. Leila runs Hoxa Gallery and is ably assisted by daughter Johan. A fourth sister, Connie, teaches drawing and painting.

Orkney artists are no mass production workers, although Sheila Fleet has a sizeable, modern showroom and workshop at Tankerness and a gallery in Kirkwall. Sheila sells online and her jewellery can be found in shops throughout Scotland. Her passion for the island environment inspires her designs such as 'Rowan', 'Rock Pool' and 'Tidal'. Sheila graduated from Edinburgh College of Art in the '60s and learned her trade with Orkney jewellers, Ortak before branching out on her own in 1993.

The Orkney family is wider than simple blood relationships. Ola Gorie, a pioneer of the Scottish craft industry, started designing and making jewellery here in 1960. Her jewellery is sold exclusively through the 150 year old Gorie family shop – The Longship – opposite the cathedral. One of Ola's early students, Malcolm Gray, left to form the very successful Ortak Jewellery. Chief designer at Ortak for a number of years was Sheila Fleet and one of Sheila's students – Celina Rupp – has since branched out on her own. Another Ola Gorie protégé was Steven Cooper who left to launch Aurora jewellery in 1998.

Andrew, Sheila, Denise, Leila and the others are not herd animals. Craft folk often want to work alone and for themselves, sometimes in quiet and stunning locations. Roger Philby, for instance, makes his Fluke Jewellery overlooking the beautiful Bay of Birsay. As well as admiring his jewellery you may be required to record your whale or dolphin sightings in the diary. A big part of the success of Orcadian artists derives from the inspiration they all get from their surroundings. The simple motifs used in the creations are so rooted in the sea and the land. They are, often, echoes of a pre-history that is still evident here.

The Craft Association supports them all, runs the craft trail, website, and helps with applications for any grants that may be available. There is an association shop in Kirkwall and displays at the airport. In fact the small, well presented showcases in Kirkwall arrivals and departure lounges are among the loveliest I have seen anywhere. They whet the appetite, just as was intended.

The Orkney Craft Association was formed during the 1980s with help from Highlands and Islands Enterprise (formerly HIDB). The trail was modelled on the Speyside Whisky Trail and the emphasis is on quality throughout. Premises, products and presentations must be maintained at a high standard for artists to retain membership of the association and keep their dot on the trail map.

Not on the trail, but well worth a visit, is Westray's Wheeling Steen Gallery, a couple of hours ferry ride or 12 minute flight from Kirkwall. The trip alone will repay the effort, with a scenic route past scattered islands.

Edwin Rendall was born on Westray in 1962 and raised on the family farm. A chance visit to a car boot sale showed him there was a lot of interest in pictures of island life and scenery so he resolved to expand his hobby, photography, and open a picture gallery, the Wheeling Steen, almost 20 years ago.

Like many islanders, Edwin had a collection of part time jobs – ferryman, airport attendant and others, as well as farming – which all added up to a full-time living. These days Edwin's son, Norman, runs the farm; his wife, Elaine operates the home baking and tea room arm of the business (wheeling steen means 'resting stone') while daughter, Rosemary, is also a photographer. Norman still calls on his dad to help with the stock as required. The crofting life is a hard habit to break.

There is something quite deep within that drives us to collect objects from afar. The Earl of Elgin brought marbles home from Greece in 1801, and an Easter Island statue was shipped to England soon after. The British Museum is full of souvenirs from abroad. I have a chestnut tree stump in my room as I write this – I begged it from a woodcutter on Colonsay, to use as a coffee table, it is my favourite piece of furniture – along with my Orkney chair.

Denise Dupres, The Orkney Woolshed

CHAPTER 27

Shetland Mainland – We don't haggle, we're British

THE SHETLAND DIALECT and accent are beautifully poetic and very different from anything you might be used to elsewhere in the UK. In every day speech they are strongest in the outer islands, in Lerwick they are more used to making allowances for incomers and visitors. When I spoke to Larry Isbister on Whalsay I could barely make him out at first but, recognising my difficulty, he toned it down. When we met Alison Simpson, however, the pair of them reverted to type. Larry said that when he arrived at Lerwick School as a young boy the playground was full of different words and sounds from all the different islands, but by Christmas they all sounded the same. Morag in the Visit Scotland office had confused her southern friends by complaining of a 'spaigie' when she first joined the running club at Edinburgh University.

The Shetland tongue derives from the ancient Norn language which began to die out in the second half of the 16th century, when judicial matters were controlled by governing Scots. Norn was, by and large, a spoken rather than a written language so quite difficult to research.

I have sprinkled a few words into the text and given you this glossary. Hope you enjoy them. Thanks to Alastair and Adaline Christie-Johnston for their excellent book: *Shetland Words – A dictionary of the Shetland dialect* (2010).

A few Shetlandic words

Aald daa	Great-grandfather
Biggin	a dwelling or a cluster of houses
Bod	a fisherman's bothy or hut; a store used for fishing requirements.
Bonxie	an great skua, piratical sea bird that dive bombs walkers if they approach nesting areas. The weather isn't the only reason to

	wear a hat in Shetland. 80 per cent of world population of great skuas live in Shetland.
Cosh	friendly
Daander	a gentle walk; to amble or saunter
Geo	a small inlet in a rocky coastline
Gloup	a sea cave whose landward end has collapsed to form a tidal pit.
Hjaltland	Shetland
Kame	a comb; a ridge of hills
Lodberrie	a house built with its foundations in the sea which combines a pier or gantry for loading or unloading of vessels.
Maallie	fulmar
Mirrie dancers	The aurora borealis (northern lights)
Noost	a natural hollow or scooped out trench to which boats can be dragged for shelter.
Peerie	small
Scooty-alan	arctic skua
Solan	gannet
Sooth mother	incomer or visitor (one who has arrived via the south mouth of Lerwick harbour)
Spaigie	a pain in the leg after exercise
Tammie Norrie	puffin

'We don't haggle,' said the young girl serving in the gift shop, on my last day in Shetland, in June of 2012. I had suggested the decorative puffin I was looking at as a gift to take home to my wife (who collects puffinalia) was a bit over-priced. Puffins are delightfully colourful creatures and my wife Bev has a huge collection now after all the islands I have visited. Even islands many miles from the nearest puffin colony will have the puffin tea towels, cruet sets, egg cups and money boxes for sale. This small bird must be worth £millions annually to the Scottish tourist industry. I think Bev likes them. It is sometimes difficult to find something different to take back – jewellery, knitwear and ceramics always go down well but I have never been forgiven for the scented-candle-in-a-tin offering of some years ago. Jane Glue, an artist on Orkney said: 'I would not have a business without the puffin.'

'We don't haggle, we're British,' the shop assistant said. 'We're

British first, Shetlanders second and Scottish a distant third,' she added. 'Oh, hang on a peerie minute, perhaps we're Shetlanders first now I come to think of it.' 'What will happen if Scotland gains her independence from the UK?' I asked. 'Let me tell you there's no way we're going off with Scotland. We'll either stay in the UK or become a Crown Dependency. Ocht, we might even join up with Norway again.'

This was late June – simmer dim in Shetland, the time of midnight sun – Shetland flags were flying everywhere as it had just been Shetland Flag Day – 21 June. The Shetland flag was designed in 1969 to celebrate 500 years since the islands had been given to King James III of Scotland when Christian I of Denmark and Norway failed to pay a dowry for the marriage of his daughter, Margaret, to James in 1469. Before then the islands had had a similar period of thoroughly Norwegian trade, language, law and way of life. The flag is a white, Scandinavian style cross on a blue ground. It symbolises the Shetland heritage shared between Scotland (the blue and white of the saltire) and Scandinavia (a plus, rather than a multiplication cross). Shetland flags and a few Union Flags flew in Shetland during my stay.

Shetland doesn't feel like part of Scotland. The accent and dialect are certainly different, with many words coming from the Norn language, and there is no Gaelic. Kilts, bagpipes and tartans are conspicuous by their absence but there are plenty of blonde Norwegian yachties in the harbour bars and restaurants. The locals and these modern Vikings seemed very comfortable with one another. I shared a pub table with ten Norwegians who were competing in a Bergen-to-Lerwick-and-back yacht race. We had steaks, watched the football on TV and then they asked if I would do a quick quiz for them about Shetland. The winner scored nine out of ten.

Islands, by their nature, involve sea crossings to reach them. Traditionally this is done by boat and I still prefer that method even when aeroplanes are available. Jim Crumley in his super book (with Colin Baxter) about St Kilda said that to reach the island on the pitching deck of a small boat was the only way to do it if you want the full experience.

I sailed from Aberdeen to Lerwick on *MV Hrossey* – one of the Serco Northlink Ferries that sail every night in each direction. It's a tea time to breakfast time crossing with the added magic of a stop in Orkney around midnight. I guess if you're a regular, commuting for business or family, then being woken up by the bow doors, hawsers, tannoy announcements and vehicle movements could be annoying. I, on the other hand, was excited to look out into the semi-darkness at the lights of Kirkwall and savour being in the northern islands again, after a whole winter of planning. I was soon back off to sleep in my comfortable cabin anyway.

Bow doors have been a worry for ferry passengers ever since *Herald of Free Enterprise* foundered in the Channel in 1987 with the loss of 193 lives. On the first trip I took after the disaster the captain used the (then) unusual form of words: 'It has been reported to me that the bow doors are secure and the vessel is ready for sea'. I guessed that the Union of Ships' Masters had probably advised him to insert the: 'It has been reported to me...' bit to cover himself against any future litigation should it turn out the doors hadn't been shut – he could not, then, be shown to have been lying or negligent. I have listened out for that announcement on ferries ever since and, as things have become more relaxed, the 'reported to me' clause has been dropped. In Aberdeen, in June 2012, the captain was confident the ship was secure. 'The bow doors have been closed,' he said.

Hrossey, and her sister ship – *Hjaltland* – have bars, cinema, cafe, restaurant and gift shop and I can never resist island memorabilia so I bought a couple of Shetland tea towels for my little camper van, some Orkney fudge, postcards and a book about local birds. I know the tea towels are not fine art and the fudge probably has no particular merit, other than a picture of the Old Man of Hoy and 'Gift from Orkney' on the packaging, but I love them. I am an island nut. My house is full of island themed ceramics, pictures, woollens and books. The worst attacks of souvenir buying are at the start of the trips, after long withdrawal, and at the end – last chance for a fix.

I showered, shaved and changed for dinner then went for a dram of single malt whisky in the lounge. The 'lads' were in the bar watching a European football semi-final but all was quiet in the lounge. I could just make out that two goals had been scored whilst I was looking at the menu. I had a lovely dish of Orkney pork, apple and black pudding for dinner in the Lodberrie restaurant washed down with simple, fizzy water (I refuse to call it 'sparkling' because it isn't). Sadly, the Lodberrie has since become the Magnus Lounge and you have to pay £18 just to sit in it.

The ferry trip to Shetland really feels like a mini-cruise. I looked out of my cabin window in the morning and watched 'solans' and 'tammie norries' heading for the colony on Noss as we approached Lerwick. There was just time for a good breakfast before rolling off to start the day in the islands. All the stress of the long drive north now forgotten.

I pitched my tent at the Clickimin camp site on the edge of Lerwick. The complex includes athletics track, swimming pool, football and hockey pitches and all the usual indoor activities one expects from a leisure centre in the 21st century. The surprise is not so much that Shetland's capital town has such facilities but that the outer islands of Whalsay, Yell and Unst – each with populations of around 1,000 – have them too. Shetland Islands Council struck a very good deal with the oil companies when North Sea oil arrived in 1975 and this paid for some fabulous roads, education, social care – and leisure facilities.

Surplus cash from the oil revenues, and there was a lot of it, was put into a charitable trust to stop central government getting their hands on it. Investments of variable worth have been made by the trustees over the years and now they are faced with their biggest challenge yet.

Wind has come to Shetland. Let me rephrase that. Shetland has always been windy – the windiest place in Britain probably, they even have to have wind-proof flaps on pillar boxes round here – but now the wind farmers have arrived to harvest it. This has the potential to be the biggest revolution in land use since the neolithic farmers arrived to till the soil and herd the stock 5,000 or so years ago. A company called Viking Energy has received government approval to install 103 wind turbines on hillsides in an area called The Kames, around 15 miles north of Lerwick.

Projects such as the wind farm always provoke intense polarisation in communities. There are the nimbys, the go-getters and modernisers, the vested interests, the apathetic, the fast buck grabbers, the conservationists and, at the bottom of the pile, the little old ladies whose houses will be blighted by the turbine towers and who don't use much electricity anyway. All of these groups are represented in Shetland over the current plans.

The Shetland Charitable Trust has a 45 per cent stake in the wind farm and stands to make a lot of money from it. Supporters claim that, as the oil money is drying up and Shetland is dipping heavily into reserves to keep the roads and swimming pools going, the wind investment must be made. They point to unemployment, dwindling population and much poorer services if it doesn't happen.

Shetland has £200 million in reserves from the oil but no new money is coming in from that source. Shetland Islands Council is currently over-spending to the tune of £38 million a year – about £100,000 per day. If the wind development didn't happen, with the projected earnings of £25 million per year for the Council, then savage cuts in lifestyle, employment and services would be the result – so say the protagonists.

One man in favour of the wind farm said 'The Shetland hills are empty. I walk my dog up there and I never see anyone. Locals and visitors do not walk the hills in Shetland – they come to see the cliff and coastal scenery. The turbines will not be blighting anyone's enjoyment.' He didn't agree with me that the whole point of the Shetland hills is that there is no one up there, that there should be places in Britain where one can walk all day and not see anyone. For every one person walking in the hills at any given time there are countless thousands who are dreaming of being alone in them, people who perhaps never go there but are simply glad they exist in their pristine state. 'No one ever goes there' is not sufficient justification for trashing something.

When the wind farm is built (and it will be built) it will still only make a small contribution to the UK energy budget. Will we need even more developments? Will we have to find more Shetland (and Orkney, Western Isles, Caithness and Sutherland) hillsides where no one ever goes? There is a proverb, attributed to the Cree people of North America and popularised by Greenpeace which goes: 'Only when the last tree has died, the last river been poisoned and the last fish has been caught will you realise that you cannot eat money'.

Can Shetland argue that the installation of 103 turbines around Voe, Nesting and Aith is reasonable because 'no one goes there' and, 'besides, they have plenty of other, unspoilt areas?' If you don't spoil it all is it OK to spoil some of it? How much is OK? When would the Cree call a halt?

I haven't found wind turbines and their towers too offensive up to now. They have generally been not too close (not to my house anyway), not too many and not too big. The Viking Energy development in Shetland will consist of 103 turbines of up to 470ft in height – four times the height of the Bell Rock Lighthouse. As a 'guideline' it was suggested the turbines be not less that 2km from any dwelling place but this has been breached in the planning. One of the very convenient things about guidelines is that you can ignore them if you like.

Opponents say that turbines will 'loom' over houses. People will be 'living in their shadows'. Whimbrel will be killed, health will be adversely affected and amenity will be lost. 'Rubbish,' say the supporters. 'They don't loom, there's no shadow, no health effects and it won't kill *all* the whimbrel.'

In the end, no one wants to see economic downturn or population drain from the islands but we don't want to lose our wild places either. I absolutely do not accept that there will be no amenity or environmental impact of the development. Morag (aged 70), who lives closest to a planned row of turbines, is upset by the prospect and may, in the end, opt to move into sheltered housing in Lerwick. She was thinking about that anyway. Should progress be held up for one old lady and a few crofters? Should Shetlanders draw a line in the peat and say 'Not in our back yard' or should they go ahead and reap the wind?

Political correctness has moved on a lot since Sir Arthur Nicolson's day (see Fetlar story – chapter 29). Not only is it no longer considered appropriate to evict people from their houses – unless you can subtly drive them out – but it's not even good to reuse bits of their houses after they've gone. At Lunna House on Lunna Ness in North Mainland Tony and Helen Erwood are restoring the roof. In fact they have embarked on a ten year programme to restore much of the listed building which is now their home. Tony called down to me from the scaffolding, when I wandered up his drive asking to take photographs, that they had bought some reclaimed slates but were concerned about denuding the decaying houses from which they came.

I was pleasantly surprised by the welcome I received. Not everyone would take so kindly to a complete stranger walking up their drive, unannounced, and pointing a camera at them. Tony, however, is used to it because Lunna House occupies an important place in the history of Shetland, and Norway, dating back to 1940. It had been requisitioned at the start of the war by the newly formed Secret Operations Executive (SOE) and was the first headquarters of the Shetland Bus, the operation by Norwegian fishermen to carry refugees out of Nazi occupied Norway and to return with supplies and agents for the resistance. Tony's parents were both members of SOE during the war so he really understands the significance of the house. A trickle of Norwegians comes every summer in a kind of pilgrimage to Lunna.

42 Norwegian men lost their lives operating The Shetland Bus. They sailed in the worst weather, at night, hoping to avoid detection by German patrols. They were not always successful however and the patrols and the weather took a heavy toll on men and boats. Apart from the practical and humanitarian relief provided by The Shetland Bus (350 refugees fleeing the Gestapo escaped that way) every Norwegian knew about the lifeline and it was an enormous morale boost for them during the darkest days of war. Nils Nesse, a very young man, was the first to lose his life when his boat was straffed by an enemy plane as they were coming across to Shetland. He is buried in Lunna kirk churchyard.

Lunna House is steeped in history going much further back than the Second World War. It stands on the site of a medieval 'haa' or hall and before that there was a Viking long house. There are also remains of an Iron Age broch dating to around 4,000 years ago. This fabulous spot – and it was fabulous as I stood on Tony's lawn and looked round at the sea, sparkling and still, in the voe below– is full of ghosts. I tried to imagine the Norwegian fishing boats anchored in the voe. I pictured the men enjoying some relief from the war with a meal and a good sleep at Lunna.

War is a terrible affliction, wherever and whenever it occurs. There are, it is said, just wars and some that are less excusable. The bravery of men like those who operated the Shetland Bus, however, should never be forgotten and it never will be. On Scalloway harbour is a fairly new monument in their honour. It was constructed from stones collected from every village in Norway that lost someone. For all our supposed sophistication as a species we still believe that a stone from one region can be imbued with more significance than any other. I think the monument builders were saying 'They gave their lives for these stones, for this land, so that we can live freely in it. For as long as these stones remain they will be remembered and cherished.' In an added touch the stones were delivered to Shetland in one of the old Bus boats.

One of the joys of travelling alone is that I get drawn into all sorts of conversations with locals. I was cooking my camper's breakfast by Clickimin Loch, just outside Lerwick, one morning when an old man cycled along and stopped to chat. He had been a child during the war and his father had worked on the shore base for the Shetland Bus (British personnel were never allowed to crew the boats for fear of blowing their cover as Norwegian fishermen). They had lived on a farm and his father occasionally brought Norwegians home for the weekend to get a bit of further respite. He told me that a Norwegian officer had come one Saturday and helped with the hay making. After the war his father told him the man had been Crown Prince Olav.

Shetland's children growing up in the early part of the 21st century do not have the threat or reality of war to worry about but there are dangers never-the-less:

'Stomach upsets and antibiotics can stop the pill working'

'A woman can pass on STI to their (sic) baby'

'If used correctly the male condom is 98 per cent effective against pregnancy'

'Chlamydia is the most common STI in the UK'

'Don't forget your contraceptives if you're going to a music festival'

These were all posters in the front window of the Shetland Youth Information Service in Lerwick. The centre isn't just in Lerwick, it's in your face. It's not tucked away in some dark council office, with a discreet sign such as (say) 'Unmentionables'. The SYIS centre is at Market Cross, at the very heart of the Lerwick shopping street, in the most prominent location in town. It's the sort of spot you might expect traders to be competing for and paying high rates.

I may be taking a huge leap in making the connection but it is typical of the islands that young people are held at the centre of things rather than to be 'seen and not heard'. At all the folk evenings and ceilidhs I have ever been to the generations mix well together. There seems to be much less of a generation gap in the islands. Whenever I've spoken to teenagers they have looked me in the eye and discussed the weather, island politics, school or football with me as an equal. There has been no hesitation or giggling. The Lerwick youngsters seemed to be making good use of their centre in Commercial Street – let's hope they were taking the advice too.

I visited a few younger children in Rachel Colclough's class at Olnafirth Primary School one morning. They had been drawn to my attention by an article in the press announcing that they had got through to the final of the Young Saltire Science Competition to be held in Glasgow. I was treated to a demonstration of the wave powered electricity generator they had made and taken to Glasgow to be tested in the wave tank at the final. A very tiny fraction of a watt had been recorded and that had been enough to secure joint second place for them. Wave and tidal energy is coming along behind wind as a renewable source and is likely to be a big deal in the Shetland Islands that these ten-year-olds will grow up in. They may not turn out to be engineers or scientists but they will always have an intuitive grasp of why renewable energy is important.

Supporters of the wind farm say that without it the Shetland population could easily fall from the current, buoyant 22,000 to pre-oil levels of 16–17,000. 40 per cent of people living in Shetland today are incomers. Shetland needs these people but also needs to be a place where its own children can have adult lives. They will often go away to university, or to see the world, but there has to be something to draw them back.

Incomers to Shetland are called 'sooth moothers' – they have entered on the boat from Aberdeen via the south mouth of the harbour. There are about 9,000 of them and they have come for all sorts of reasons. Some will have come to work in the renewable energy field. I hope some of the Olnafirth children get their engineering degrees at Edinburgh or Aberdeen then come home to join them.

Sadly, when I visited in 2013 I found the young people's centre closed.

Katya Moncrief, Shetland.

CHAPTER 28

South Havera – Uninhabited but not abandoned

LERWICK IS A delightful town. The harbour pubs and bars are welcoming in a traditional and time-honoured way. If you're feeling trendy you can enjoy a super lunch, behind plate glass windows on the first floor of the brand new museum. You can look out over Hay's Dock while you savour homemade fish cakes and fine wine. Island nuts, however, will understand that, delightful as places such as Lerwick are, the Holy Grail for aficionados is an uninhabited island.

Places that have been lived on in the recent past, or maybe one with a tiny, isolated human community can be the most fascinating. My plane to Foula conked out on the runway on my first day in Shetland. A part, and an engineer, would have to be summoned from the south so my hopes of reaching Britain's most islolated community were put on hold once again. Magnus Gear, the heritage ranger on Foula had laughed when I told him Foula had been on my list for years. 'That's what everyone says,'he said. Once again I would not get to see the Kame or the Gloup. That was in 2012, in 2013 the plane was grounded by the mist so I still haven't been to Foula.

It was an inauspicious start to the trip and the weather was not looking too clever for the boat ride to South Havera (pronounced Hayvra and spelt Havera by locals but Havra on modern maps). John Tulloch had put me in touch with Frank Charleson who put me in contact with John-Lee Fullerton, who had a fast peerie boat at Bridge End, between East and West Burra. John-Lee's mum owns a part share of South Havera and various friends and family run a couple of hundred sheep on the island.

John-Lee did that long intake of breath through his teeth, the sort plumbers and builders do just before they tell you it's going to be expensive. 'It's not looking too grand for Saturday,' he said. 'Phone me at 9 o'clock on Sunday morning.'

I lay in my tent early on Sunday and thought the wind and rain sounded pretty much as they had done the night before. I couldn't sleep any more so got up and went to photograph buildings in Lerwick. Then I hit on the plan of turning up at John-Lee's house, rather than phoning, thus making it more difficult for him to say no. The plan worked and by 9.15 I was drinking coffee in his kitchen and looking at photos of South Havera.

I must have seemed pretty mad, desperate or both because John-Lee said we could try it and we set off for the harbour. Robbie-Lee, John-Lee's ten-year-old son, ran ahead when we got to the pontoon, and climbed into a 10' boat that was half full of rain water and looked as though it had been built from an old wardrobe. John-Lee spotted my hesitation. 'Don't worry, that's Robbie-Lee's boat he uses for pottering round the harbour – I built it from an old wardrobe – we'll be going in this one,' he said, indicating a much sturdier craft on the next mooring.

We made South Havera without any difficulty. It has always been my experience that skippers like to over-estimate sea conditions, maybe out of bravado but more likely out of that caution and healthy respect for the sea that men need in places like Shetland. We moored the boat off a tiny shingle beach in a tiny geo called Nort Ham on the east side of Havera. It was silent, apart from the cackling maalies on the ledges. I've heard these birds on the ledges of every deserted cove, on every deserted island I've ever been on. Their sound echoes round and intensifies the silence.

The census of 1891 records 24 people, living in four families, but the last ones left in 1923. It had been a strong community, with a school teacher and eight pupils. The teacher lived in a one-up-one-down cottage, teaching downstairs and sleeping upstairs. Adalene Fullerton – whose father, John Robert Jamieson, was one of the last to leave the island when he was eight years old in 1923 – told me the last school teacher was probably her uncle James. Teachers of small island 'side schools' could work without formal qualifications if they took a basic test. The school house is still there, minus roof and floors, but I was able to look out through the tiny window down to the beach at West Ham below and across to the cliffs at Point of Skeo Geos. As a school teacher myself I used to look out of my window and dream about being in places like this – I wonder what teachers on South Havera dreamt of.

Havera is a fertile little island of just 150 acres. The islanders couldn't afford to waste the productive ground across the centre so they built their *biggin* on the stony ground, on a narrow promontory between two geos. There was no peat for fuel so this had to be rowed across the mile of open water from Deepdale, on Mainland to the east. They had no bull either so semen had to be shipped across the sound by rowing boat as well. This was in days before artificial insemination, however, so the receptacles used for the transport were the cows themselves. The females requiring service had to be rowed, one at a time, to the Mainland bull at Maywick – a job traditionally done by the island women.

Robbie-Lee's *aald daa* had lived on South Havera until, at the age of eight in 1923, his family decided to leave. The other families had quit the island a few months earlier and life became too difficult for one family to stay on alone. Robbie-Lee is a keen family historian and eager to tell me about the women rowing for peats, to the bull and to market in Scalloway.

The sea route from Havera to Scalloway is about nine miles, almost due north up Clift Sound between East Burra and Mainland. It is a mostly sheltered passage, once you have crossed a mile of open sea north of Havera. The Sound is only a few hundred yards wide and protected from just about everything apart from a north wind. It would have taken them about four hours in a 20 foot open boat. If conditions were good they could sail it in an hour.

I can only imagine the pleasure of arriving in Scalloway, perhaps at mid-day on a warm spring Saturday. Would the women have been dreading the effort of rowing all that way, or would they have been keenly anticipating 'a day out in town'? Scalloway is hardly a metropolis. There would have been friends and relatives to visit – they may have stayed overnight but Adelene thinks not: 'In the summer there would be too much work at home to do, and in winter such trips would be few and far between,' she told me. There might have been a few new things in the shop to tempt them. A pony and trap or motorbus ride into Lerwick would, probably, have been out of the question. 'In any case shops in Scalloway would have been just as extensive as those in Lerwick at that time,' Adelene said.

The Havera folk would have carried knitted goods and eggs to trade for tea, sugar and paraffin in town. The woollen items would have been loved by today's tourists in search of authentic, local products. The wool was entirely grown, washed, spun and knitted on South Havera. The Shetland wool comes, naturally in a range of colours so would probably have been undyed.

In the end the community on South Havera decided to leave. The history of human population there ended in 1923, just as it had on many other islands, and would do on others within a few years. Depopulation would continue throughout the 20th century. There is a critical mass of population needed to keep an island open for business and once numbers fall below this it becomes impossible to sustain a settlement. It was around this time that other famous island desertions occurred: Mingulay in 1912 and St Kilda in 1930.

Robbie-Lee's great granddad and his family had wanted to stay on South Havera but, once their friends and neighbours decided to leave in 1921, their position became untenable. There would simply not be enough able bodied people to help with the boat, peat digging and a thousand other tasks in this labour intensive existence.

The sea-girt way of life is still in the blood of modern Shetlanders though. Robbie Lee's little boat – *Da Dey* – is named for an old South Havera fiddler, of some note, James (Dey) Jamieson. I was impressed by the trust and confidence placed in Robbie-Lee by John-Lee and Linda, his mum. 'He has set limits on how far he can go up the Sound with his boat,' said John-Lee. 'Every year we move them back a bit. There's a peerie beach he can visit with his pals if he wants to. He has a life jacket and he knows, absolutely, that the first time he messes about with the boat it will be taken away.' I saw little likelihood of this young man 'messing about'. As soon as he gets home from school each day he is pestering his dad for work on the croft. The land and the sea are still very important here.

Voe boat, Shetland.

CHAPTER 29

Fetlar – Three sea-crossings away

IN THE INTRODUCTION I mentioned that islands can take one, two, three or even four sea-crossings to reach. Most of the three- and four-crossing islands are now uninhabited but Fetlar, at three crossings, clings on (Scottish mainland to Shetland Mainland; Shetland Mainland to Yell; Yell to Fetlar).

Martha, the RSPB warden on Fetlar, waved her arm at the expanse of cliff and coast scenery and said 'Fetlar's great, there's no marine development here.' By that she meant no salmon cages or mussel beds anchored in the voes and firths. Neither are there wind turbines, nothing to spoil the view. Pretty as this is, there's a downside. Fetlar has a population of about 50 and, in recent years, has been a community struggling to survive. There is one shop which gives access through a hole in the wall to The Cosh Cafe. The cafe opens 11am to 4pm but the owners of the joint premises only allow the shop to open 11am to 1pm. Both are run by the same couple. I had lunch at 1.30pm, for which I had to walk through the dark and empty shop. After my toasted sandwich I walked back through the deserted shop, escorted by the waitress/shopkeeper and enquired about making some purchases of supplies for dinner, only to be reminded it was closed. It would not open again until 11am the next day, by which time I would have sailed for Unst, the next island. Please note: I was standing in the shop, with the assistant, and she had nothing else to do.

A lot of council time, money and effort have been put into supporting Fetlar. A breakwater has been funded which, it is hoped will re-energise in-shore fishing and allow the ferry to berth overnight. There are those in the council and elsewhere, however, who are sceptical of how much difference it will all make to the future on this beautiful island. With business models like the one in the shop/cafe it is hard to disagree.

Birdwatchers have always arrived on Fetlar in steady numbers. For many years it was home to a snowy owl, a bird that should really have been in the Arctic but seemed to prefer Shetland. Today the star birds are the red-necked phalaropes and the red-throated divers. I was sitting quietly looking for the red-necked phalarope on Funzie Loch (pronounced 'Figgie' for some unaccountable reason) when my attention was drawn to a camouflaged figure, crawling on his belly to the water's edge across the other side of the loch. He was pointing a lens the size of a dustbin (the old fashioned sort that dustmen carried on their shoulders, not a wheelie bin) across the loch. I followed his gaze with my binoculars and easily spotted the phalarope. It was a male, not as brightly coloured as the female, but a delightful bird for all that. Unusually among birds the male incubates the eggs so has the more cryptic colouration for concealment at the nest. Red-necked phalaropes have a fine, black bill, dark face and white throat. The bright red neck, especially on the female, gives the bird its name. In Britain they are found only in the far north, so I have been lucky to see one.

Buoyed by the spotting of my first ever phalarope (a life tick in twitcher parlance) I headed off for a *daander* round the south east headland of Fetlar – known as the Snap. It's marked as a footpath on local maps and strategic stiles across fences made progress easy for the five-mile walk which ended, conveniently, back at my accommodation.

I sat to ponder by a tiny lochan and was treated to a pair of red throated divers with their single, black chick swimming behind. Through the binoculars I could see the effort the chick was making to keep up. Its feet were paddling so hard they were breaking water astern and leaving quite a wake. They say that if you see a red-throated diver you have probably already disturbed it so I moved away quickly and quietly. The short viewing was enough to make the day.

I stayed in the fantastic little house at Aithbank, on Fetlar, which has been adopted by the Shetland Amenity Trust as a camping böd. A böd was a seasonal house used by fishermen during the season in days gone by and the name has been adopted for these 'camping barn' style buildings. Shetland has nine böds (the first one opened in 1992 and more are planned) and they are all in buildings of historic significance. Using them as böds helps preserve them, as well as providing super budget beds for hippy travellers like me.

Aithbank was the former home of local bard and storyteller James John 'Jeemsie' Laurenson (1899–1983). It is a traditional, stone two-up-two-down house with an out-house for the facilities – which are never-the-less very clean and modern. Inside the kitchen is well equipped, if basic, and the other room has a peat burning stove. There are bags of peat in the porch. I lit a fire on the chilly spring evening and watched the tide come into the bay down below. At bed time I settled into the box bed upstairs and recalled some writing by Orkney poet – George Mackay Brown – about the deep luxury of a box bed in a house at Rackwick. My nearest neighbours, with their single, twinkling light, were half a mile away.

I had brought my tent to Shetland and was enjoying a mixture of wild camping and council facilities but the böds were hard to refuse. At only 20p a night more than the camp site at Lerwick the comfort levels were much higher. You do have to share your böd (not your bed) with whoever turns up but 'bödders' are generally like-minded folk – even if their washing up sometimes leaves a bit to be desired.

One glorious evening, during the simmer dim, I walked the two miles along the north-east cliffs to the remains of Gruting Round House. The house had been built by Sir Arthur Nicolson during the 19th century as a weekend retreat from his more imposing and palatial Brough (pronounce broch) Lodge, overlooking the sea at the west end of Fetlar.

I won't get into the Nicolson family tree but suffice it to say there were four Arthurs and the last member of the family – Lady Jean Nicolson – quit Fetlar sometime in the 1980s. She retired to Edinburgh and Brough Lodge fell into disrepair (a major restoration project is currently underway, however).

Fetlar was acquired for the family in 1805 with Brough Lodge being built around 1820. In 1826 Arthur Nicolson became Sir Arthur when he revived a baronetcy which had lain dormant. Whether he thought his newly exalted position put him above his fellow men or not is unknown but, over the next 20 years he cleared the land of its inhabitants in as savage a fashion as any in Scotland. The more profitable sheep took their places.

The area of Lambhoga had been cleared of its families in 1822 and now Sir Arthur took the east end in 1839–40. The north was cleared in 1847 and the area around Brough Lodge was evacuated in 1850–52. Today the habitation is limited to Tresta and Houbie in the south, and a few people in the north-east.

Gruting Round House is little more than a pile of stones now. The outline of a large, walled garden remains and a couple of decorative pillars hint at it having been more than a simple dwelling. It is said that it was built from the stones of empty houses after the people were cleared from the land. Their ghosts, apparently, proved too much for Sir Arthur and he stayed only one night in the place.

I caught the first ferry of the day to Unst the next morning. One Fetlar resident catches this 07.50 crossing each day, for the half hour trip and 20 minute drive to Baltasound on Unst where she opens her restaurant. The building had been closed by the owners (who live in Australia) but the council persuaded them to let someone open it for the summer rather than have it boarded up and unwelcoming. A mystery benefactor paid the rent and insurance for the season. If Marie, the chef, can get cleared up by ten to nine each evening she catches the last ferry home to Fetlar, otherwise she has to stay with her son in his house on Unst. There's a former end-of-terrace council house for sale at £56,000 next door to the restaurant which Marie is considering, as well as possibly buying the restaurant.

My baked haddock was good, the dining room was airy and nicely furnished and decorated, the view of the blue sea (which lapped 20 yards from the picture window) was priceless and the dinner prices were very reasonable. There were just three of us eating however (there's seating for 30), prices were not advertised and no starter was offered. Another business model it is difficult to see a future for. I ordered a single malt in lieu of a starter and then Marie realised she could offer me a small portion of crab (one of the other main options) as a starter so I ordered that – it was very nice.

Baltasound is almost at the end of the road. After that there is Saxa Vord, where someone has occupied an abandoned RAF camp, stuck a canvas banner and a string of bunting across the gatehouse and called it *Saxa Vord Resort*. The bunting and the sign make the entrance look only slightly less like Check Point Charlie than, well, Check Point Charlie. You can, however, get a very nice dinner there. I guess if you are a group of birdwatchers, walkers or just island nuts like me, and you just want somewhere to eat and sleep then it's OK.

Beyond Saxa Vord Resort are the incomparable sea cliffs at Hermaness National Nature Reserve. Superb views of *maalies*, *solans, tammie norries and bonxies* can be had and, if you're lucky, a *scooty-alan*, along with Muckle Flugga lighthouse just beyond. Muckle Flugga is not quite the northern most tip of The British Isles, that distinction belongs to Out Stack, a lump of guano covered rock a few feet further north still.

CHAPTER 30

Whalsay – Shetland's fishing capital

ON MY LAST DAY in Shetland I packed the tent, beside the loch at the north end of Unst and drove down for the 07.05 ferry to Yell. I tagged on with a mini-convoy of other vehicles and we whizzed south at 50 to 60 mph. Timing had been perfect, the ferry ramp was just dropping as we arrived and we rolled straight on. No one got out to look at the view they'd seen so many times before. They just got on with chatting, dozing or putting finishing touches to make-up. With the short crossing of Bluemull Sound over, the ramp at the other end of the boat lowered and our convoy sped up the hill to cross Yell. 50 to 60 mph was maintained (Shetland has fantastic roads – paid for from oil revenues) as we dashed to meet the Yell Sound ferry for Mainland.

I dropped out at Voe to catch my boat to Whalsay but the others dashed on. Only one had stopped on Yell and I assumed the rest were pressing on to the capital. Unst to Lerwick would be at least a two hour trip requiring two sea crossings and 57 miles driving. Although employment in Shetland is very high there are, clearly, a few who have to make sacrifices to maintain it.

Whalsay is Shetland's fishing island – a big part of their commercial trawler fleet has always been based here. Today there are about seven of the biggest, smartest, most powerful – and most comfortable – of fishing boats to be found anywhere in the UK.

In 1923 the island of Whalsay, on the east side of Shetland, had a population of just under 1,000 (today it is close to 1,100). At almost 5,000 acres it is 30 times bigger than South Havera and wholly different in its ability to sustain its population. The problem of how you get to the shops in Lerwick, however, has always exercised the minds of Whalsay folk just the same.

I went to see skipper Davie Hutchison of MV *Charisma* to hear about his life at sea. Davie picked me up at the pier and soon had the kettle on at his 'Southfork' style ranch house at the top of the hill, overlooking the whole of the harbour at Symbister.

'We didn't get ferries here until the 1970s,' said Davie. 'If you wanted to go to Mainland there was a peerie open boat you could borrow. When we went to sea we always had a few women aboard wanting a lift to Lerwick – and the same coming back. There was a steamer that came up from Lerwick about three times a week, went round all the northern isles of Whalsay, Fetlar, Yell and Unst and back again. It carried everything – freight and passengers. We managed fine. When the ro-ro ferry arrived, with its multiple daily sailings we said it would never have anybody on it but now you have to book because it gets so full.'

Davie went away to sea a few days short of his 15th birthday, in 1960. The tradition was that you joined as cook and progressed to deck hand after a few years. 'Yes, the crew did get some poor food at times but as long as they got plenty they didn't complain. They helped me out a bit as well. We were all taught to cook properly at school and at home in those days so it wasn't so bad. I suppose my apprenticeship lasted eight years because in 1968 I took a half share in a scallop boat with a pal. The Highlands and Islands Development Board (HIDB – now the Highlands and Islands Enterprise, HIE) gave us a loan. Then in 1979 there were nine of us bought a boat for over £1 million. In 1995 the group was down to seven and we got a bigger boat. Now we have yon *Charisma*.' Davie nodded over his coffee, way down to the harbour to the sleek, bright yellow super trawler tied up at the pier.

Crewman Larry had shown me over *Charisma* the day before and you would have to see it to believe it. 'I've seen all the episodes of *Trawlermen*.' I said to Larry as we climbed the gangway. 'Is it like that?' 'Aye, pretty much.' He said. I reported that conversation to Davie later on and he almost choked on his biscuit. 'I can't believe Larry said that, he's been kidding you on – I've no seen so much drama in a year as there is in one episode of that programme.'

The first thing I saw on *Charisma* was the trough of brightly coloured house plants, set on the parquet floor, against the etched glass screen and just below the cut glass decanter and whisky tumblers on their silver tray. The deep leather sofas faced the 40" television screen and the video library was to one side.

Through the glass screen the dining room had 14 places and gave onto the fully equipped kitchen that would not have been out of place in the Dorchester. After dinner each crew member could retire to read or watch TV in his own suite (lounge, bedroom and ensuite). I didn't see the skipper's quarters but I guess they were, perhaps, a little more comfortable. In fact one problem on boats like this is that, because the crew can be so private and comfortable, the camaraderie can suffer. 'You sometimes only see a crew mate when you are called to work or for dinner,' said Larry.

The bridge was like that on *the Starship Enterprise* – no, really, it was. There was so much room to walk around between the seats, screens, hydraulic control panels and printers that the builders had installed a sofa and coffee table to one side, simply to fill up the space. 'The bridge didn't need to be that big,' said Davie, 'but it would have looked silly on a boat that size if they'd have built it any smaller.'

I commented that *Charisma* was so clean. 'Aye, well, we only go to sea about six weeks in the year. It's all we need to catch our quota – so there's plenty of time for cleaning and no much time getting dirty,' said the skipper.

Someone had told me he had been asked to go as relief crewman on a trawler once. 'We shot the net, trawled for a few hours, filled the hold and then came home. We were only away two days. A couple of days later I got a cheque for £10,000. I assumed it was a mistake but the skipper said: 'No, that's your share of the catch.'

After my visit to Davie I caught the 5.45pm boat back to Mainland and sat in the queue watching 20 or so big cars carrying people in suits off the boat. They were coming home from their shops and offices in Lerwick. They were commuters, just like commuters in Putney and Barnes. Whether they consider themselves part of the rat race I didn't enquire.

Dog on dive boat, Shetland.

CHAPTER 31

Voe – A floating shed in the harbour

SHETLAND IS JUST about as far away as you can easily get and still be in the UK (I know that Shetlanders will say they are not far away, it is London and Edinburgh that are remote – but you know what I mean). It is a sea kingdom. Travelling any distance in Shetland soon requires a water crossing. Place names derive, more often than not, from bold geographical features: Baltasound, Olnafirth, Sullom Voe, Whale Firth and Herma Ness. These places are all defined by the sea.

You can come here to get away from it all if you wish. Some people do that very successfully and others get driven back by the first winter. James, the postman from England, working on Fetlar, has what many would-be escapees might call the dream job, but was having difficulty coming to terms with the six day week which means it's hard to get to town. The ex-lighthouse keeper at Muckle Flugga, on the other hand, loves the isolation so much he bought the flat in the shore station when the light was automated and he became redundant. His wife and family still live in the south.

Guido, another incomer, had had a tough time elsewhere and came to Shetland to lick his wounds. He fancied building a boat and asked around if anyone would be prepared to lend him a shed. There was, as it happened, a disused fish farm shack floating on a raft in the firth so he borrowed that.

When I arrived at the pier on a quiet Sunday afternoon I was amazed to see a couple of hundred people. They were occupying every vantage and staring out to sea. I tried to see what they were looking at, thinking there must be whales or dolphins in the bay. In fact they were all watching the little hut, which had been strung with Shetland bunting alongside flags from Guido's native Belgium. The double doors opened at one end of the shed for Guido and friends to push a perfect Viking ship, off the raft and into the water.

Guido had gone round every house in the area to invite them all to his launch. They gave three cheers in time honoured fashion and then repaired to the Pier Head Bar for refreshments. 'It was just a tree when he took it into that shed,' someone said.

CHAPTER 32

Harnessing the wind

STEPHEN HAWKING, during the preparation of his book: *A Brief History of Time*, was advised that every equation he put in would halve his readership. He settled on just one in the end, and even that was dropped from a subsequent edition. There will be no equations in this story, and I will limit the applied physics to just this: a one bar electric fire needs a kilowatt. A megawatt is a thousand kilowatts, a gigawatt is a million kilowatts, and James Watt was born in Greenock, Scotland in 1736.

They tell us that to make progress as a planet we must harness more and more energy. Our current nuclear and coal power stations are wearing out so we must find replacements (Britain will lose 20 gigawatts of electricity generating capacity by 2015). Other people tell us that burning fossil fuels, such as coal and oil, adds carbon dioxide to the atmosphere and this causes global warming and this is a bad thing.

Nuclear power stations on the other hand are environmentally friendly, until they go wrong that is, and until you have to find somewhere to dump the waste. There is a huge drive to develop alternative energy sources that will not pollute the environment or run out – the so-called renewable energy supplies – and these include wind farms, tidal barriers, wave power and others. Scotland currently produces 500 megawatts of power from renewable sources (mostly wind).

So, should we be building wind farms on Scottish islands? If we knew all the equations, did all the maths and considered all the aesthetics and politics we could probably arrive at the right answer for planet Earth, but that achievement is beyond me. All I can do here is have a look at how the wind movement stands in some of the islands at present.

Turbines are ugly things to some people, although I don't find them too bad in small numbers. They have a futuristic, quiet serenity about them. They are gentle giants. They change the landscape but we shouldn't necessarily hold that against them, farmers, foresters and builders have been doing that for thousands of years. David Bellamy himself once told me that the beautiful Derbyshire Dale in which we were standing, with its varied flora and fauna, is only that way because of human tinkering. The landscape we are so jealous of today is only the product of our interference in generations past. Britain was once covered with trees, which farmers tore down, so it is not a pristine territory, although cutting down trees contributed to global warming in the first place.

There is even a specific precedent for changing an island land-scape with man-made wind-harnessing structures. Centuries ago the St Kildans covered their Hirta hillside with stone sheds or cleits. The cleits had gaps in the walls letting the wind blow through to dry the puffin and fulmar meat hanging inside. The islanders had built what they needed to survive as comfortably as they could in their difficult environment. In all the literature I have read about St Kilda I have not seen any suggestion that cleits are eye-sores, some may think so, but most see them as part of the St Kilda story, and I am certain the thought never occurred to the people who built them or collected supper from them.

In a recent visit to South Havera, Shetland, I saw the remains of a windmill that had been built to grind the island's corn. The mill was never successful and the island was abandoned in 1923 – but the mill was another precedent.

There is a lot of thought being given to generating electricity using wind, because of its green credentials. Scottish islanders are taking a keen interest because wind power is particularly suitable for their small, often remote (and often windy) communities. Fair Isle, Gigha, Unst and Tiree, among others, have some very elegant wind solutions to their energy problems. Big boys from across the water have also started eyeing the potential of islands with plenty of wind, and land, to build huge commercial wind farms from which to export electricity to the national grid. Proposals for hundreds of turbines, spanning an area the size of London, on Lewis in The Western Isles have been turned down but replaced by smaller pro-posals.

Fair Isle installed the first commercially operated windmill in Europe, a 60kw tower, in 1982. They are called turbines really but I noticed how island folk call them windmills. I think this says a lot about their feelings for them – gentle, rustic, homely things. Linda Grieve on Fair Isle called it 'an old friend'

After some initial teething problems the original Fair Isle windmill became profitable, justifying the installation of a second, 100kw tower some time later. Between them now they supply more than half of the island's need. The shortfall is made up by two diesel generators linked, not by the almost inevitable computer, but by the original, 1980s relays and timers to the turbines.

The whole island has been supportive of the project. It gives them cheap, clean electricity and so any reservations about noise from the blades (there is a bit when you are standing close to them) or visual intrusion on the landscape are easily accepted. Tourists seem more fascinated than offended by them and the birds don't seem to mind. The warden at Fair Isle Bird Observatory said: 'They turn quite slowly and the birds seem able to avoid them. We do check round the base occasionally but never find any corpses.' There have, however, been reports of bird casualties, especially eagles and wildfowl at larger wind farms elsewhere. The RSPB was concerned for the sea eagles and golden eagles on Lewis had the farm gone ahead there. Wildlife organisations are similarly concerned for whimbrel on Shetland.

The diesel generators on Fair Isle guarantee a supply to the islanders from 7.30 in the morning to 11.30 at night. If you are watching a late film, and it isn't windy, well then you miss the end and go to bed by candlelight (this was a romantic part of my stay on the island and the locals had laughed at my suggestion that we could video the rest of the film).

When the wind starts to blow the first bit of wind-generated electricity is sent down a heating supply cable, to storage heaters and the water heater in each house. As the wind strengthens the windmills start to supply lights and sockets too, and at this point the generators are turned off automatically until the wind drops. Each householder has an indicator light that tells whether the supply is coming from the diesel or the windmills at any given moment. In this way they can, in theory, choose whether to put the washing machine on at 13p a unit, or wait until the wind blows and do the laundry for just 5p a unit. In practice, of course, the cost just evens out over time.

The electricity that comes from the windmills down the heating cable is even more attractively priced. Any units over 3,000 per quarter are free. In this way the homes are heated for a maximum price, which is fixed each year, no matter how cold it gets. This may seem wasteful but we have to get used to the idea that the energy is free and clean so, no matter how much we use it does no harm. Free wind energy also encourages islanders to use less coal, which they still do for topping up and 'because you can't beat a coal fire at times'

Wind energy is so environmentally friendly that producers are subsidised by government, through Renewable Obligation Certificates. There are even times when the turbines generate more than can be used so it has to be 'dumped' to keep the supply stable. Large 'heat sinks' or 'dump banks' are heated up using the surplus electricity and heat is dissipated to air using fans (generally, however, 98 per cent of electricity generated on Fair Isle is utilised).

The small island of Gigha, just off the west coast of Kintyre, has three windmills which the Gigha Heritage Trust bought second-hand from a farm in Cumbria in 2002. The turbines are the Vesta 27 model which Andy Clements, Gigha's wind manager, described to me as the 'Morris Minor of wind turbines – old but reliable.' I also noted that, just as in the second-hand car trade, the Vestas were described as 'pre-commissioned' rather than 'second-hand' It reminded me of the 'pre-owned' car I had once bought and the 'pre-loved' little black dress my wife got from a dress agency.

Unlike Fair Isle, Gigha is connected to the national grid. It is barely a mile from the mainland, rather than the 24 miles of North Sea between Fair Isle and Shetland. All the electricity generated on Gigha is sold to the grid and the islanders buy it back in the normal way. The plus for Gigha is that cash from the sale of their wind is being used by the Heritage Trust for a major house refurbishment being carried out right across the island (The Gigha Heritage Trust was set up to manage the community buy-out of the island a few years ago, following a model similar to the one used for the purchase of Eigg from its absentee landlords).

With the trust owning the land on which the turbines were erected, and the local quarry that supplied the aggregate for the base, as well as buying bargain windmills, the project on Gigha has been profitable. There is even talk of Gigha's partnership with mainland energy companies being able to arrange cheaper electricity for local enterprises, such as the fish farm, as the Trust seeks ways to maintain the viability of the community. We may even see

the day when Gigha becomes an energy provider in its own right –
like Powergen only smaller.

What cachet there would be then for environmentally aware
types, at dinner parties in Chipping Sodbury or Putney, being able
to say 'All our electricity comes from wind turbines on a tiny little
Hebridean paradise called Gigha you know.' As the renewables
movement grows we could have consumers buying from places
such as Gigha, in much the same way as we specify 'fair trade' coffee when we visit Starbucks for our double tall, skinny lattes.

One of the issues generally with electricity generation is that you
can't store it – although Fair Isle did, once, experiment with an ex-
Edinburgh, battery powered milk float (electricity generated surplus
to immediate requirements could be used to charge up the batteries
on the float). On Unst, in The Shetland Islands, the PURE project
(Promoting Unst's Renewable Energy) is looking into the use of wind
to power the generation of hydrogen gas which, of course, can be
stored. The gas can then be used to release energy via fuel cells as
required. They even had a hydrogen fuelled car running round Unst's
roads to further test the feasibility of the venture. One other beauty
of burning hydrogen as fuel is that there is no carbon dioxide given
off, only water vapour, so it doesn't contribute to global warming.

Wind farms fall into two categories. There are the 'smallholdings'
such as the one on Fair Isle, and there are huge complexes such as the
one planned for Shetland. We should consider each one on its merits
and not be seduced into thinking all wind farms are good (or all bad).
For small communities a single turbine can make a big difference. It
can provide a large percentage of the energy needs, at low cost, and
any impacts on the environment are easily reversible. The community can decide for itself to put up with any slight noise or loss of
view if it sees that the benefits outweigh these disadvantages.

On Lewis, however, there was much more local opposition. There
were two proposals, from two different companies, and they planned
to have around 300 turbine towers between them, each one higher
than the Forth rail bridge. It would have been the largest on-shore
wind farm in the world, needing 167km of new road, millions of
tons of concrete and electricity pylons marching all the way across
to Stornoway. There would be risk of peat fires, injury to rare birds
(this is sea eagle country) and loss of wild, wide open space.

The towers would have stood within sight of The Stones of

Callanish – one of Europe's most significant Neolithic treasures. All the electricity would be exported to the mainland grid and, although locals would be compensated, they would have much less control over the project – all of the disadvantages and only some of the benefits. Proposals such as these are much harder to swallow. Of course big farms produce a lot of meat. Lewis could generate 700 megawatts (three quarters of a gigawatt) almost five per cent of the UK projected shortfall. Conversely, if everyone turned off their TV standby lights when not viewing, then we wouldn't need so many turbines.

Any future, significant wind turbine development on the Outer Hebrides would depend on the provision of an interconnector – a £400 million additional cable link to the mainland through which to export the power. The extra generation of electricity, by wind, wave or tidal means, would have to be big enough to underwrite the cost of the interconnector. All installations could then send their power through the cable.

Wave and tidal power are still in their infancy and so large, on-shore wind turbine installations would be needed. Work has already started on 39 turbines at Eishken on Lewis that will each provide 3.6 megawatts. They should be ready for connection to the grid in 2015. The Pentland Wind Farm will have six turbines providing three megawatts each. There are smaller, community projects planned too. Stornoway Wind Farm, on Stornoway Trust property, is awaiting consent for a 150 mW installation. The community will have a 20 per cent stake plus an annual community benefit package worth about £4,000.

The massive development of 160 turbines will never happen now. The environmental (some would say NIMBY) lobby has killed it off – even if the interconnector was to arrive. Renewable energy is the future but perhaps, in the islands at least, it will have to be small scale and very much more energy efficient.

As a society, we are beginning to turn our attention seriously, and at last, to our use and abuse of the planet. It is a complex problem, not one that will be solved by turning off a few light bulbs or putting up a windmill, but it can be done. It needs to become a cause celebre. It needs to be fashionable to walk or cycle, recycle, insulate, turn off and turn down. Air travel produces a lot of carbon dioxide, so how about taking the train up to the Kyle of Lochalsh for a holiday on Skye this year or to Aberdeen for Orkney and Shetland or Wemyss Bay for Bute, instead of jetting south.

I wonder what James Watt would think of all this fuss? He could be credited with starting the industrial revolution in Scotland and, I suspect, he would derive some satisfaction from his countrymen now leading the way in the turbine revolutions.

Faith, Hope and Charity, Gigha.

CHAPTER 33

Out Skerries – An island
of no importance

SKERRIES ARE, INDEED, a long way out from the centre of things, even so far as the rest of Shetland is concerned. Lying an often bumpy ferry ride from Mainland they are not in the mainstream of the life of these most northern islands. Actually 'out' is a corruption of 'east', but the locals just say 'Skerries'.

I arrived in a full gale on-board the ferry, *MV Filla*, after a two and a half hour passage up the east coast of Mainland from Lerwick, the Shetland capital. *Filla* is named after a small, uninhabited island in the Skerries group. She was built and launched in Norway to the general amusement of the shipyard workers there for, whilst *Filla* means 'hill' in Shetland it means something else in Norwegian. When asked why they were all laughing after the name had been revealed at the launch ceremony, one worker explained that *Filla* means 'a thing of no importance' in Norwegian. They just didn't think it was a suitable name for a boat – or an island.

Our course took us past Whalsay, where the ferry crew all live, and, before that, the tiny islets of Peerie Fladdicap and Muckle Fladdicap. 'Peerie Fladdicap is the half-way home point on a trip from Lerwick to Whalsay,' said the skipper, Peter Irvin and, although these men are all seasoned sailors, I thought I detected a note of relief in his voice as we past the Fladdicaps that we were getting nearer to safety. I had been reading about Betty Mouat, a 19th century Sumburgh lady who was travelling by boat to Lerwick one day when the entire crew had been lost overboard. She drifted for eight days on this very same grey, heaving sea until she washed up safe in Norway.

All good sea-farers hear these stories and develop a healthy respect for the sea, knowing that there is a fine line between a safe passage and disaster – and the crew of Filla were no exception. I had asked the skipper if I could ride on the bridge, pleading sea-sickness and the need to be able to see the waves coming and the horizon, but Shetlanders are so warm and welcoming that he took

no persuading. I was treated to a running commentary about the
Shetland Bus, minke whales, variable pitch propellers and bonxies,
all whilst viewing from the comfortable vantage of the left hand seat.

Forget Alton Towers this was the ride of a lifetime. *Filla*, with
raised prow ploughing forward, was in her element. I know she
had no option but to sail down into the deep troughs, with waves
up to the wheelhouse, but it was as though she had chosen to go
there – on her own terms. I have rarely felt so elated and safe at the
same time. At the lighthouse on Bound Skerry, *Filla* turned beam on
to the waves and held station in the boiling sea until the skipper
judged the precise moment to release the handbrake and we surfed
in through the north mouth, between a rock (Lamba Stack) to starboard, and a hard place (Angry Head) on the port side. In the next
moment we were in the total calm of the beautifully sheltered natural harbour between the islands – Grunay, Bruray and Housay.
Filla turned sharply past the tiny islet of Trollsholm before settling
easily against the pier.

The harbour is safe in all weathers and provided a good base
for the Shetland *haaf* fishing industry in times past but in spite of
this security, skippers still have to know their way in. The approach
to South Mouth (we had arrived through North Mouth because South
Mouth was currently too shallow) appears as a blank cliff wall until,
at the last moment, the narrow channel opens. A bullion ship, the
De Liefde, came to grief here in 1711 and occasional finds of coins
are still made. The big strike was in 1967 when a chest of silver coins
and gold ducats was recovered. Smugglers also made very effective
use of the rugged coastline's caves, arches, channels and geos.

Out Skerries lie just over 60 degrees north (the same latitude as
St Petersburg and southern Greenland) and tourist outlets in Lerwick
even offer souvenir certificates for travellers that have made it this
close to the Arctic Circle. The islands are the most easterly in Shetland
and this makes them (like their more famous neighbour Fair Isle)
a prime site to see migrating birds during spring and autumn. Bill
Oddie has been a regular visitor and has said that Skerries are as
good as Fair Isle for the chance of seeing rarities, but he wants to
keep them to himself so hasn't publicised the fact (sorry Bill). Small
breeding colonies of gulls, terns, eider ducks and black guillemots
(tysties) litter carpets of sea-pink in the summer months.

Some island communities acquire a languid, *laissez-faire*, almost 'hippie' outlook but not so the one on Out Skerries. There is a real determination to continue living here and to thrive. In recent years the salmon farm has closed in response to falling prices, but the new worker/islander cooperative is planning to reopen with a more viable organic product. *Filla* is designed with two big fish holds to support the enterprise and, when the South Mouth of the harbour is dredged, she will be free to come and go in almost any weather – choosing whichever 'mooth' is least like a whirlpool spa at the time. 'The salmon farm has to work,' said one shareholder 'If we don't want another St Kilda on our hands, it has to work.' Already, since the earlier closure, some people have to travel to Lerwick to work during the week and the community cannot sustain such a fragmented existence indefinitely.

Out Skerries boasts the smallest secondary school in Britain. There were four primary and two secondary pupils taught by a headteacher and her staff of one full-timer plus assorted peripatetic specialists. If there are no nursery children in any given year, as this year, then the sandpit can be put away and the screen pulled across to provide additional science space for the older ones. Schools are at the heart of all the island settlements and without them young families will not stay and new families cannot possibly settle. Without the youngsters to carry on the work and traditions of the communities they will simply die of old age. As I was writing this chapter I heard that Out Skerries' school had closed temporarily, following a dispute between the school and the islanders. Proof, if proof were needed, of the fragile nature of such communities. In March 2014, the secondary department is closed permanently.

George Henderson, the Skerries shopkeeper, was in hospital during my stay on the island but his friends had organised a rota to keep the shop open. The morning shift was out meeting the ferry when I arrived but there was a note pinned to the door saying 'Back soon'. I went in and wandered round the deserted shop, making my selections supermarket style. No baskets are needed, you just stand in the middle and pile things up on the counter which is never more than arm's length away. Luckily all the prices were marked so I was able to leave the correct amount and be on my way.

On subsequent visits to the shop there were staff on duty but I discovered that the notice on the door was a permanent fixture – a bit like SALE notices in department stores. The islander behind the counter was clearly motivated by good business practices, and full of sales jargon: 'Come again.' She said, which I felt was a little unnecessary as it is one of only two shops on the island. I took advantage of their free 'left shopping' service – you leave your bag of purchases and then when they close the shop they hang your bag on the door knob outside for you to collect at your leisure.

Fresh drinking water is a hard won commodity on tiny islands such as Out Skerries and on my walk around the hill I came across an open gutter, neatly tiled and running spirally down and round the hillside. The idea being that water runs off the flanks to be collected in the gutter and channelled down to a reservoir. It was rather like the system for collecting rubber from trees.

I finished my walk around Bruray and then collected my things from the shop door a couple of hours later. There used to be a similar arrangement on Kerrera where a crofter would have a bottle of Islay malt left in the telephone box at the pier by anyone returning from an Oban shopping trip. On one occasion the bottle remained there, quite safe, all weekend.

Davy Johnson has lived on Skerries all his life – including 35 years at the fishing and boat building. In the early '80s he spent two years building a 38 foot fishing boat – *Searcher*. She was clinker built of larch and was his pride and joy. 'I always wanted to prove to myself that I could do it.' He said. The whole island turned out for the launch in 1983 followed by a feast in the community hall.

Searcher made a good start at the fishing but then in 1984 she struck the rocks on a neighbouring island, in fog, when the self-steering gear failed. Davy found himself sitting on the side of his wheelhouse in the dark. He put out a mayday and the Lerwick lifeboat responded promptly but, even here, the principle and tradition of self-help dictated that a local boat found him first and, with his son one of his rescuers, he was winched to safety just before midnight.

The community try to get together at least once a month in the hall for a social gathering of some kind. The highlight is the dance and supper that follows the annual fishing competition or *da eela*. Whatever is caught provides the supper. Shetland community events such as this are very inclusive of young and old alike. A mainlander was telling me about *Up-Helly-Aa*, the most famous of all Shetland festivals. He said that youngsters are included in such celebrations and grow up with them, taking increasingly responsible roles as they do. He offered the opinion that this was an important factor in teaching them how to behave in society. It seemed obvious when he put it like that and maybe this is something we have lost in our big cities.

The gale blew over and *Filla* returned a couple of days later so I had to leave Out Skerries, sadly, as it meant I would miss Sunday lunch with the whole island in the community hall – perhaps another time. There is evidence everywhere you look on Skerries, and with everyone you speak to, of the determination to go on living there: drinking water tapped from the hillside; boats built and lives clung to when they go down (even now Davy is battling the wind and salt to make things grow in his garden, planting one thing as a screen for others). Friends rally to run the shop and men build walls in Lerwick Monday to Friday while they campaign to re-open the salmon farm. Teaching is juggled skilfully in the school so that young families don't have to leave. An island of no importance? Not to Skerries folk it isn't.

CHAPTER 34

Fair Isle – Walking with binoculars

I WENT TO FAIR ISLE to see what all the fuss was about. After several years of bird-watching at the local reservoir where there is often not much about (Bill Oddie once said of his local patch: 'I was off down the reservoir again, to count the tufted duck'). I thought I would treat myself to a week of Rolls Royce twitching to see if it was as good as everyone made out. I was already an island-going aficionado and so the prospect of a spring visit to Fair Isle held much appeal.

Fair Isle is in the premier league of island destinations, easily up there with St Kilda, Staffa and the like, but if you are just starting out on your voyages of discovery you will need to know that Fair Isle lies roughly half way between Orkney and Shetland. It is about three miles long, lying roughly north-south, and approximately one mile wide. The land slopes down from the high red sandstone cliffs at Ward Hill in the north, to the low, southern coastline and the so-called South Harbour.

The population of about 70 all live in the fertile, cultivated land in the south, which is separated from the hill grazing towards Ward Hill by Hill Dyke and Feelie Dyke which bisect the island. The island folk, like all thriving island communities these days, have good communications with larger neighbours. An eight-seater plane arrives most days from Shetland Mainland to the north. The mail boat – the *Good Shepherd* IV – plies the two and a half hour crossing to Sumburgh on the southern tip of Shetland, carrying passengers and supplies. The internet, radio, telephone and fax are all used here, to great effect, to run businesses and simply to keep in touch with people elsewhere.

Fair Isle gets a big tourism boost from the influx of birders who stay, mostly at the observatory (newly re-built and re-opened in 2010), but also in bed and breakfast with the locals. Serious twitchers can be a bit isolationist – flying in from The Scilly Isles to see, say, a chimney swift and then out again on the next plane, without so much as buying a postcard in the shop – but us 'walkers with binoculars' like to take our time and get the full flavour. Ian Mitchell in his book, *Isles of the North*, says that, increasingly, visitors to the obs (birder jargon for observatory) are not hardened bird watchers but 'empty nesters' wanting a bit of peace and quiet in an unusual location. For that reason the trustees applied for a drinks licence – so you can now have an impertinent little cabernet with your clootie dumpling and custard.

David and Susannah Parnaby run 'The Obs' as a joint enterprise of scientific bird monitoring and guest house. You most definitely don't have to be a twitcher to stay here, although most visitors do have some interest in wildlife. David and Susannah are just as happy to take you on an evening puffin walk, peregrine chick viewing or serve you a pint of Skull Splitter, as they are to explain the identification of a red-flanked blue tail. You stay full board and dine on excellent food at a sociable, refectory style table. There are three choices each evening: take it, leave it or vegetarian. There are also self-catering and B&B available.

I walked away from the Britten Norman Islander, down the track to the road and there, within minutes of my arrival, was a bluethroat, a gorgeous little bird, a bit like a robin with a blue bib half covering its red breast, skulking along in the bottom of a ditch. I couldn't believe it – a life tick so soon – I had never dreamt it was going to be this easy. I thought that, at least, I would have to spend several hours searching.

A life tick, by the way, is seeing a bird for the first time, and ticking it off in your list. The observatory has a bookshelf full of birding reference works for visitors. There is a contributions box – the Tick Tin – at the end of the shelf and the deal is this: For every life tick you collect during your stay you give 50p to the library. If, however, your life list is already in excess of 200 bird species you must give more, on a sliding scale up to £20 per tick for the really top birders with lists over 500. It says on the bottom of the Tick Tin that it was started in 1959 by Michael Wills and Jeremy Sorensen. The same receptacle, a Nescafé tin, is still in use.

That first day, in late May, was brilliantly warm and sunny and, apart from the bluethroat, there were willow warblers and chiffchaffs everywhere. There were spotted flycatchers hawking from fence posts after flying insects, a garden warbler and a brilliant red-footed falcon just before bedtime. Like the bluethroat, the lightning quick falcon is only a visitor to our shores and the last thing its prey sees are the bright red talons and an equally bright red patch around each eye.

With the wind freshening in the south-east the next day I was alerted to a hobby that had been seen near the north lighthouse so I trekked up the track before lunch in search of it, and took the opportunity to have a look at the Stephenson lighthouse at the same time. Fair Isle might be small by metropolitan standards but it still feels like a long walk up through the moorland to the north end. I had thought the locals might have got a bit cramped after a while on the island. I wondered if they ever hankered after some-where different to go for a walk perhaps, but I was soon put right by one octogenarian lady who told me 'I have lived here all my life and I have never been as far as the north lighthouse.' During the day I dipped on (failed to spot) the dotterel but ticked black red-start, pied flycatcher and dipped on the common rosefinch in the bushes just outside the shop.

There are all sorts of politics and ethics in bird watching. There are horror stories in less well regulated hotspots about gangs of twitchers dragging chains across fields to put up birds that are thought to be resting there, so they can be seen. Ian Mitchell reported an occasion on Fair Isle (pre-enlightenment) when a red-necked grebe was chased on the water to exhaustion, just so it could be caught and ringed. The grebe was found, dead, on the beach the following day. An old hand had told me: 'Shake the bushes outside the shop, the rosefinch is often resting in there and you might wait for ages to see it otherwise.' To be fair this was the only example of political incorrectness I encountered – I don't count the high ranking British Trust for Ornithology man who advised me during one walk with binoculars 'If you thought that was a thrush nightin-gale, it was, so tick it in your book and let's press on.'

It should also be remembered that many of the rarities we see on Fair Isle are there because they have been blown off course by easterly winds and bad visibility due to fog or rain. Many will have already perished in the North Sea, and those that make it may feed and rest up only to give out during the onward migration, north or south depending on the season. The even rarer American vagrants, whilst delighting the birders, stand even less of a chance. So, hoping for easterly winds and a good influx of birds is not very politically correct either. We really should be happy with clear skies and a steady, southerly air stream in the spring, to help the birds on their way to the breeding grounds. Beware what you wish for.

Being a schoolteacher I was, naturally, interested in the school on Fair Isle. It caters for primary grade children and, like most small island schools, ships them off to the mainland for secondary education. Numbers fluctuate because of natural movement of families in and out of the island, one family with three children of primary age can decimate or save an island school, depending on which way they are flitting.

I sat having coffee with the school dinner lady. I had actually been surprised to find her, in a fully equipped kitchen, cooking a hot lunch for the children. She explained: 'It may seem like a small island to you but it is still a long way for children to walk home for lunch, especially with the winter weather we get here at times.' I can't remember what they were having – I think mashed potatoes featured – but I recall it was a nutritionally balanced and tasty meal. On top of which they would all sit down together and eat in a civilised, sociable fashion, placing their knives and forks correctly at the end – a marked contrast with some big city school south of the border.

It's not only the unusual birds that get people excited on Fair Isle. Birders are incurable listers, the over-arching list, for every birder, is the life list, containing every species you have ever seen, anywhere in the world so long as it was in the wild (you can even count birds you have positively identified by their call, without actually seeing them, so you can all go and add cuckoo to your life list immediately). Then there is the year list (January 1st is a big day in the calendar because every bird you see on that day will be a new tick). You could have a garden list; British or European list. Some birders spot birds on television and look out for things in the background in western films or Michael Palin's trip through The Himalaya for example. One birder, also a keen rock climber, started an abseiling list, to which he added all the birds he spotted whilst coming down the rope at the end of a climb. Which brings me to the two ladies I met on Fair Isle. They were having a lovely week, walking with binoculars, and had set about compiling a Fair Isle list. They had reached 49 and were due back on the plane that afternoon. 'What we wouldn't give for a wood pigeon round about now,' One of them said. 'We can't move for wood pigeons at home, but where are they when you need them?'

I did not shake the bushes outside the shop to scare out the rosefinch. I spent half an hour there every time I passed but it never appeared. Perhaps it had moved on or perhaps it had been a false sighting in the first place. On one occasion I joined a line of birders with their 'scopes all set up and pointing into the middle distance. 'What are we looking at?' I enquired. 'Shore lark.' came the casual, almost grudging response 'In that long grass'. I trained my embarrassingly new telescope as coolly as I could manage on the grass and peered through it. We watched for a bit before another birder joined the line next to me. 'What have we got?' he asked. 'Shore lark – in that grass over there.' I said, trying to sound professionally unexcited. The newcomer scanned the grass for 30 seconds and then, stepping back from the line, addressed us all with authority: 'Is anyone on this bird at the moment?' There was silence in the ranks. 'Has anyone actually seen this bird in the last hour?' he continued. We all shuffled uncomfortably from one foot to the other. 'Ach, bloody amateurs,' he said, and walked off.

Since my visit an extension to the breakwater has improved the situation, especially for the summer months. The ferry can now lie in the water more safely between trips. The pier is in North Haven, separated from South Haven by a narrow strip of beach and sheltered by Bu Ness which is almost a separate island. A mile further south is Sheep Rock, a towering stack which is, again, almost detached from the island. With space at such a premium on a small island, sheep were carried up to the grassy plateau to graze and fatten each year. The only way up was to climb a chain that had been anchored at the top for the purpose – it was tested by the first man up each year. Stewart Thomson told me he used to climb the chain when he was much younger. 'We could only get about eight ewes up there,' he said. 'We did it for the adventure more than anything.'

The weather for the entire week was brilliant – sunny, breezy at times but warmish for the time of year and everyone trooped down to a grassy raised beach at the south end one evening after dinner for the Locals v Visitors football match. I played in goal for the away team and a more beautiful setting for the beautiful game would be hard to imagine. Forget San Siro or The KC Stadium, this was the ultimate venue.

A grassy bank formed one touch line where the spectators sat, and the pitch sloped gently down to the edge of the beach at the other side. Goal posts were fashioned from driftwood with scraps of discarded fishing nets – crossbars sagged in the middle, where they were jointed. I have travelled to many isolated spots in Scotland and I have noticed that, no matter how remote, there are, invariably, three man-made structures: a lighthouse, a war memorial and a football goal. During lulls in the action I looked around me and knew, with absolute conviction, why I come to places like Fair Isle.

You might even be lucky and catch a ceilidh with *Fridarey*, the local folk group, playing. I caught them at the Shetland Fiddle Frenzy one year and they brought the house down in the final concert on Bressay. A band of brothers, sisters, parents and daughters they typify the strength of family and community on Fair Isle.

The observatory has impromptu entertainments in the evening, if there is anyone around who can offer one. There was a slide lecture on *Cetaceans in Britain* and another on *The Arctic*. During the days there were: red backed shrike, golden oriole, black redstart, turtle dove, long eared owl and whimbrel (I can't see a whimbrel without thinking of Howard and Marina in *Last of the Summer Wine*. The lovers had gone to a bird hide in the latest ruse to find seclusion: 'Oh Howard'. 'Oh, Marina, I think we've just heard a whimbrel') I sat for hours on the cliff top in the evenings and watched the puffins. Before finally leaving Fair Isle I had to pay £5.50 to the library fund for my 11 life ticks. They were worth every penny.

David and Susannah took over as wardens at the observatory in 2011 and have recently contributed a second child to the Fair Isle community – helping to secure the future of the school as well as the observatory. They would love for you to go and stay with them, or just pop in when you're on the island. Phone 01595 760258 or email: fibobooking@btconnect.com. More details can be viewed at www.fairislebirdobs.co.uk

CHAPTER 35

Cramond Island – The acceptable face of global warming

ELEVEN THOUSAND YEARS AGO, give or take, the land we now call Scotland was frozen under half a mile of ice. No one lived there. There were no plants or animals. The notions of Scottish nationhood had not been dreamed of, but the land was there, waiting to be freed from the big freeze and for the story to begin.

Before going any further I should say that people had lived in Scotland during the Paleolithic period, in the milder climate *before* the last Ice Age closed in, but they left very few traces.

When the ice melted for the last time the rich soil was exposed and then colonised, first by plants, then animals and eventually by people. It was a period of global warming but, instead of creating problems for Earth's human population, it was a period of opportunity as virgin territories were made available in the north.

Where the first 'Scottish' people came from is not certain. It would seem likely that some walked from England – although it would be thousands of years before anyone called it that – possibly up the Tweed valley. At first they might have been hunting parties following game but settlement could soon have followed.

Some may also have moved along the coast in dug-out canoes. There were no roads or tracks and the sea was often the most accessible highway. There are parts of the Scottish mainland, still, in the 21st century, which are easier to get to by water. The communities of Ardnamurchan, Morvern and Knoydart in the west go by boat to do their shopping. As I write this a landslip blocking the road at Strome Ferry has necessitated car ferries being brought in to ply up and down Loch Carron to bypass the blockage.

There has been a long association between Scotland and Ireland. It is only about 15 sea miles between the two countries at the nearest point. Famously St Columba brought his Christian message from Ireland to settle, eventually, on Iona off Scotland's west coast. It may be the very first people came to Scotland that way which might explain why there are so many Mesolithic traces on islands such as Jura, Islay, Colonsay, Oransay and Rum.

People have made some pretty impressive sea crossings in seemingly impossible craft. It could be that people crossed from Ireland in dug-out canoes. No such boats survive in Scotland but they have been found elsewhere in Europe. Henri Macauley, folk musician and artist on Gigha, told me recently she had just crossed to Rathlin Island, Northern Ireland, in a 20 foot open boat for a folk festival. It had been six hours each way and a great thrill. There was something in Henri's voice that told me this was a much bigger thrill – and deeper satisfaction – than six hours in a car, bus or train would have been. People who live by the sea have it rooted in their psyche. The vestiges of that need are still expressed by trips 'doon the watter' on old ships like PS *Waverley*.

It has also been suggested that so many Mesolithic sites have turned up on west coast islands, rather than on the east coast, because the land in the west has been relatively less disturbed by modern agriculture. One or two cynics complain that archaeologists just like spending their summers on Hebridean islands and so make more effort to work in such places.

Radiocarbon dates show, quite accurately, that the ice melted some 11,000 years ago but the first people didn't arrive until 1,000 years later. The land would have been very hospitable long before that however, plant colonisers would have moved in straight away and a mature, mixed deciduous forest cover would have been established in places in perhaps as little as 100 years.

It is thought that Mesolithic hunter/gatherers, who had been well established in England and Ireland long before this time, had not yet developed a mature maritime culture. They simply didn't have the skill or confidence, at first, to travel north in their dug-out canoes and coracles.

Also at that time there was still a land-bridge across what is now the North Sea and some incomers may have arrived from north-western Europe by that route. Tantalisingly a single flint scraper was recovered from the bottom of the North Sea 90 miles north-east of Shetland. There are a number of ways it could have got there but, could it have been dropped by someone walking from Dogger Land to the newly available hunting and gathering grounds of Scotland?

There have also been a couple of flint arrowheads discovered on the island of Stronsay, Orkney. They could be 10,000 years old, as could charred hazelnut shells discarded near the tidal Cramond Island on the Firth of Forth. Mesolithic travellers may have stopped here for lunch and forgotten the country code. The ice melted from north-east Scotland first so it is no surprise that Cramond and Stronsay have revealed two of the oldest bits of evidence of human presence discovered so far.

I walked over to Cramond Island in 2012. It was a glorious summer day and I followed the tide out as it exposed the concrete walkway built to service war time defences placed there. The tiny islet of just 19 acres is partly wooded and there are the remains of an old summer house. The view from the 68 feet summit takes in the Forth Rail Bridge, Inchcolm Island, the Edinburgh skyline and, on a really clear day, way out up the Firth of Forth to the Isle of May and Bass Rock.

I had gone to Cramond in the belief that the ancient hazelnut shells had been found on the island but the local historian I met corrected me and said they had been on the mainland nearby. Even so, during my customary reverie on the island, I sat and imagined the hunter-gatherers on Cramond. They surely wouldn't have walked by without exploring it. Their view would have been pretty similar to my own, minus the bridge and tower blocks. It is a lovely place for a picnic but do, please, be careful if you decide to wander over. People get stranded every year and one unfortunate baby[1] was washed away by the incoming tide when the pram he was travelling in floated off the causeway.

The period we are talking about is referred to by archaeologists as the Mesolithic or Middle Stone Age (roughly 10,000 to 6000 years ago). It was a time when humans led a nomadic, hunting and gathering existence, rather than by agriculture in settled communities. They didn't yet build stone houses, tombs or stone circles so they left very little evidence of ever having been here. Archaeologists, with unbelievable amounts of patience and determination however, have sifted through tons of soil, sand and debris to piece together the best picture they can of how Scotland's first arrivals lived.

The Mesolithic folk were nomadic to an extent because they had to follow the seasonally available nuts, fruits, fish and game. They probably moved around a home territory however, perhaps with a base camp and several seasonal camps that were revisited each year.

Smaller 'work parties' may even have been sent to gather a particular harvest and carry it back to the group.

The need to move around easily, together with the ready availability of fish and shellfish made coastal locations popular with Mesolithic people. A number of camp sites have been found on islands and, since this book is about islands, I am confining the discussion to those sites, although there were plenty by the sea and rivers on the mainland.

Some of the oldest known evidence for human habitation in Scotland is found on the tiny, Inner Hebridean island of Oransay (see earlier chapter). Oransay is a tidal island, attached to its larger neighbour, Colonsay, by a sandy strand which makes a pleasant walk at low tide. Today Oransay is an RSPB reserve managed and farmed for the benefit of the wildlife. It is a beautiful place on a sunny day, with *machair*-covered dunes, a low hill and sandy beaches.

Oransay has been the subject of intensive excavation on the dunes where a number of shell mounds or middens have been discovered. What appear to be nothing more than a few grassy humps are, in fact, huge piles of 'kitchen waste' from Mesolithic settlement. Having hunted or gathered their shellfish, fish or birds the chefs simply tossed the waste onto ever increasing piles. Some very painstaking work on Oransay (on the ear bones of fish found in the middens) has shown that each of the five shell mounds was probably used at a different season.

People have tended to assume, because the middens are dominated by shells, that shellfish was the staple diet at that time. Anyone who has enjoyed a plate of mussels, however, will know that the pile of shells is much bigger than the meat. Furthermore, why would anyone chew through a bowl of rubbery limpets if fish, lobster and game were in plentiful supply? On the contrary, it appears that our Mesolithic ancestors enjoyed a varied, tasty and nutritious diet which also included seabirds, eggs, nuts and fruit.

The ice melted 11,000 years ago and within 500 years there was a good coverage of birch woodland with hazel, elm, pine and oak. That vegetation was enjoyed by deer, bear, elk, wolf, boar, beaver and auroch (a type of ox). It was a fantastically well stocked larder for a very small number of people. The reindeer, woolly rhinoceros and mammoth, sadly, did not survive the final glaciation. Still, we mustn't be greedy.

Tools that could have been for leatherworking have also been found and so, although they didn't have stone houses, they may well have been very comfortable in hide tents with wooden and bone frames and, perhaps skins and furs on the floor for insulation. The early islanders had fire, fuelled by wood, dung, dried sea-weed and, perhaps whale bone at times. They had clothes, beads and necklaces. Although bows and arrows have not surfaced from this period in Scotland they did exist elsewhere in Europe and so we believe our people had them.

If we assume they were cosy and snug in their shelters through dark nights and stormy days, and that on good days they would be busy hunting and gathering, preparing hides, making clothes and tools then it sounds like a pretty good life. There was plenty of varied food and although a hunter/gatherer lifestyle cannot sustain a large number of people it is actually easier than farming (which came later). They would have had some free time.

At night there may have been lamps with animal fat in bone vessels and some light from the fire. They were anatomically fully modern humans, just like us. Modern people who have gone off to live in Iron Age settlements, for a year or so as an experiment, have reported on their return to 'civilisation' that they could not tolerate the heat in most modern buildings. They had got used to the outdoor life and so it is easy to believe the Mesolithic people lived comfortable lives.

When the temperature dropped and the gales blew in from the Atlantic – and they can blow for days and weeks at a time in some winters – they would have had family life of games and story-telling; planning and reminiscing to sustain them in their shelters. They had fully modern brains and so we must assume they had a rich language and culture, which may have included poetry and music. They may even have recorded or illustrated things on, say, bark in forms of 'writing' and art. Traces of ochre have been found and evidence from Europe suggests they would have had art in some form.

I sat by one of the Oransay shell mounds on a warm, spring day and tried to imagine a Mesolithic life there in the winter – but could not, because I think I lack the Mesolithic psyche. Steven Mithen, in his book *To the Islands* and Caroline Wickham-Jones in *Fear of Farming* both suggest the hunter-gatherer still resides in all of us, however. They argue that humans were hunter-gatherers for most of their two million years on Earth and won't have lost the inclination from the gene pool just yet. I think mine is seasonal.

I thought my Mesolithism might be weather dependent but then I had another go at it. I stayed for a few days in a bothy on Mingulay. The island is uninhabited and I had it to myself. I had shelter, fuel, food, water, clothes and bedding. I had candles and a book and was supremely content.

Our islanders probably lived in extended family units of 10 to 12 people, perhaps including grandparents. Several families may have come together for celebrations, nut and fruit harvests. There would be opportunity for exchange of news, barter and finding partners. The genetic imperative must have required an incest taboo in human societies since the beginning. Young people would have had to look outside their immediate family for a partner so jamborees and festivals would have been vital.

There would have been many interesting artefacts of human life lying around a Mesolithic camp: tools; clothes; hides and timbers from the shelters; bone tools and jewellery and perhaps even coloured material. Much of this was organic and so has not survived in the acid soil which predominates in Scotland.

I wonder what our ancestors from 10,000 years ago aspired to, as they lay in their shelters at night, or day-dreamed while collecting fruit, preparing a hide or paddling a canoe by day. They had no metals or plastics, let alone machinery so it would have been impossible for them to fantasise about a machine to power a canoe, say, or a device to cut firewood. They may have longed for more live births; less child mortality; a cure for toothache (abscesses have been identified in a few remains); to see what the next island was like or, perhaps, to see their daughter again after she went off with a bloke from another group.

It has been suggested that stones might have been placed around shelters, where the hide met the ground, to act as draught excluders. I wonder if any thoughtful camper ever put one stone on top of another. If so, was this the start of stone house building? My Uncle Norman was a 20th century bricklayer and his maxim was 'If you can lay one brick, straight, on top of another, then you can build a house.' Caroline Wickham-Jones, on the other hand, told me the Neolithic was more about farming than it was about stone houses.

Stone houses are prominent on Orkney but in wooded environments there is sufficient shelter from the wind without them.

In the end, the Mesolithic folk died out. Their place was taken by the swanky, new incomers with their farming technology and big ideas about living in one place, corralling animals and growing crops. These were the Neolithic men and women, who did not take kindly to people hunting and gathering all over 'their land'. In Orkney they built stone houses, tombs and stone circles. Perhaps they were saying: 'Look, this is our land because our grandparents lived here.' There may have been a few upwardly mobile Mesolithic types who adopted the new culture – they may have even married into it – but it is generally thought they were usurped.

Note

1 He was rescued quickly and without injury.

CHAPTER 36

Inchcolm – An island at the crossroads of time

I AM FASCINATED by Scottish island history. I try to imagine what it must have been like for the first people to settle in Scotland – the villagers at Skara Brae in Orkney, for example, going about their limpet collecting and bere baking 5,000 years ago (bere is an ancient variety of barley, grown only in Orkney today). I have stood by the Bronze Age burial chamber on Inchmarnock, and wondered who gave the young woman the jet necklace she was wearing 3,000 years ago; and I would love to have been to a ceilidh in Village Street, or to the strangers' gallery for a sitting of the St Kildan parliament a hundred years ago.

One autumn day I took a boat trip from South Queensferry, under the Forth Rail Bridge, and over to the tiny island of Inchcolm. It was late October, the last trip of the season for *MV Forth Belle* and there was only a handful of us on board. The air was breathless, the sun scorching and the sea calm – a jewel of a day. The sort of day I normally look for in early spring, when the sea sparkles and the islands thrill with new life and warmth after the long winter. On this day, however the custodian on Inchcolm was packing up for the winter and preparing to leave the island the next day.

This tiny sanctuary stood on a crossroads in history. The story goes that a hermit was living in a crude cell on the island when, in 1123, King Alexander 1 landed to shelter during a storm. The hermit sheltered the king and the king, in gratitude, pledged to build a monastery on the island. Alexander died in 1124 so it fell to his younger brother King David 1 to establish an Augustinian priory on Inchcolm. Born in about 1084 David only missed Macbeth by 30 odd years – from this distance, of nearly a millennium, they seem almost contemporary. Inchcolm was already a much sought after, if pricey, burial plot before David arrived and Shakespeare has Macbeth say:

Sweno, the Norway's King, craves composition;

Nor would we deign him burial of his men
Till he disbursed at Saint Colme's Inch
Ten thousand dollars to our general use.

In his youth David spent time at William's court in England, and brought a lot of modern, European practices to trade, money, town planning, justice, local government and the church. He introduced the feudal system in Scotland – and he built a lot of monasteries.

An actual contemporary of David, a man born of Viking stock, in the west, was *Sumarlidi* – the summer raider – better known to us now as Somerled. As Inchcolm Abbey was developing, Somerled was styling himself 'King of Argyll' and he ruled over that county, including all the islands, with a firm hand. In the early 1130s. Alexander's illegitimate son, Mael Coluim, rebelled against David's rule, and had Somerled as a powerful ally. David may have had to call on the support of The English King, Henry 1, to quell the uprising, but quell it he did. When Somerled died, just 11 years after David, his sons divided the vast island territories between them: Donald and Dougall founded the great clans of MacDonald and MacDougall – The Lordship of the Isles was in the making.

David rarely ventured north of the Forth. He lived especially in Roxburgh and invested a huge amount of time energy and money (his silver mines allowed the development of a modern cash economy) in the building of abbeys, monasteries and priories. His Selkirk Abbey was moved to Roxburgh to be just across the river from his castle at what is now Kelso. He supported a Benedictine monastery at Dunfermline and made grants to Edinburgh, Berwick and Stirling. There was also support for Holyrood and Melrose – the best known of his abbeys. He wanted to add York to his portfolio but never quite managed it.

David 1 patronised the Augustinian order, it is said, because he wanted the kind of clergy who could best undertake the reconstruction he wanted towards his economic miracle. Augustinians were a reformed continental order, sharp eyed entrepreneurs and particularly hospitable. It may be more than a coincidence that their abbeys were often close to royal palaces, the better to take advantage of the dinner, bed and breakfast trade. Cistercians were also favoured for their agricultural and business acumen. They were 12th century property speculators. We may never know if David was more interested in the hospitality than the spiritual services.

The corporate networks of these organised communities could tap into commercial systems of mainland Europe. The monks of Thiron, in France were granted free access for their ships to any part of David's kingdom for trade. The Scottish monks took advantage of this to buy French wine and sell their own agricultural surpluses. David's new silver coins would have oiled the wheels of this trade admirably.

Inchcolm Abbey is, and was in David's time, a short, easy boat ride from the palace at Holyrood in Edinburgh. I wonder if the dignitaries there enjoyed an evening sail for dinner, conviviality and a lie-in before breakfast at the island sanctuary. It would certainly have been exclusive and an opportunity to de-stress from the pressures of government. Security and privacy would have been guaranteed – no paparazzi or terrorists likely here.

A French merchantman may have been riding at anchor in the lee of the island and Scottish nobility could have been wined and dined on board, or the captain brought ashore for dinner in the abbey. No doubt the abbey wine cellar would have been restocked with brandy, and the sailors could have gone away with fresh meat.

It is not known whether pilgrims to or from Iona passed this way although Inchcolm has been called The Iona of the East, and some references have been made to its dedication to St Columba. Travel then was principally by water and so, rather than be an out-of-the-way spot, Inchcolm would have been more accessible than many places. Travel from Iona would not have been out of the question.

The most illustrious resident of Inchcolm was Walter Bower, Abbot of the community from 1418 until his death in 1449. Bower is best known for his History of Scotland from the 11th to the 15th century – *Scotichronicon* – in which he gives some insights to the life of the island. Unlike the present guardians, who vacate Inchcolm in the winter, the Augustinians fled the island in the summer months when they were vulnerable to sea-raids from the English. Bower says:

> When the stormy winter weather was at hand and the corn gathered into the barn and the fear of English raids less menacing, the abbot and the bretheren, together with the servants and all their gear, went into residence on the island.

The Inchcolm abbey started as a simple church, it was expanded several times and built up into an abbey with accommodation for about 20 canons plus visitors. By the time of Walter Bower's incumbency the Abbot's residence was quite comfortable – in modern parlance it might be described as a first floor apartment with sea views. It was in a private wing with all rooms facing the beach and, with a nod to community living, the Abbot shared the latrine block with which his flat joined onto the communal dorms. The idea was that the tide came in under the latrine twice a day and flushed it but, with falling sea levels since the 12th century, it is now high and dry. I suppose global warming might see it operational again.

There are very few pointers to how the canons lived at Inchcolm – a wash basin set in the stone wall, with water supply above and drain below; a bowl or cresset basin in which a light would have floated on oil. Above the cloister is the dormitory, with a stair to the church for night services and one for daytime use. My favourite feature is the warming house in which the monks kept a good fire during the winter. I suppose it was a sort of lounge, or common room in which, I like to think, they might have dropped the piety for a while and talked of worldly things – the weather, the harvest, visitors to the abbey and perhaps their own aches and pains. I wonder if they ever went as far as to moan about the Abbot's latest initiatives, the price of European wine or the spitting, crackly quality of the firewood the merchant had supplied them this time.

So, there it was, this tiny speck of land at the crossroads of the new, feudal, medieval Scotland. William the Conqueror was still alive and kicking in the south. Somerled was sowing a great dynasty that would become The Lordship of The Isles in the west. The northern Vikings had had their day, but only just, and free trade with Europe, as more and more foreign ships came up the Forth, was growing.

In the introduction to his book 'David 1' Richard Oram says: 'He brought a rough edged and barbarous kingdom face to face with the cultured smoothness of European civilisation. Scotland's medieval history, it seemed, started with this man.'

David died, peacefully in his bed, in his castle in Carlisle in 1153. His body was carried to Dunfermline Abbey for burial, the cortege crossing the Forth at Queensferry. The water had been rough when they arrived on the southern shore but, as soon as the coffin was placed in the boat, it was stilled. The entourage had a calm passage, in sight of Inchcolm all the way, just as I did.

Epilogue: Still island-hopping
after all these years

IF YOU'VE READ THIS FAR and would like to comment on anything in the book I'd love to hear from you. You can contact me at richardclubley@hotmail.com. If you've spotted any typos, errors of fact or omission please let me know. If you just want to share your own island going stories I'd like to hear them.

The fascination with islands still burns in me as strongly as ever. I'd still love to visit North Rona, the Shiant Islands, Flannan and a few others. Further afield I'll bet the Falkland Islands, St Helena and Easter Island would each repay a visit.

I am looking into the possibility of renting an island house somewhere. The plan is to rent out our home in Sheffield and spend a year living the island dream. I'm hoping that my wife will take to it and agree to a permanent move, but one step at a time.

On Arran, last summer, I was bugged all holiday with the view of Pladda – a super little island just half a mile off the beach – but I couldn't persuade anyone with a boat to take me. In the end I borrowed a plastic kayak off a bloke on the beach and paddled myself there one very still, early morning.

As I reached Pladda the water shallowed and I could see, first the kelp, then the bottom. The black, rounded boulders were still wet from the ebbing tide and the thrill when the boat bumped and scraped between them, before coming to a silent halt, was fantastic. I had been at sea for half an hour.

Pladda is tiny and uninhabited – the best kind of island – apart from a bothy used as a holiday hide-away by the owner. There is a lighthouse but, as with all Scottish lighthouses, this is unmanned and controlled from a house in Edinburgh. Walking was difficult since there had been no sheep, cattle or people to tread desire lines in the tall grass around the edge of the low cliff. The remains of several sea urchins were scattered on the beach from an otter's breakfast.

Pladda with Ailsa Craig in background.

Further Reading

Atkinson, R, *Island Going*, Birlinn, 1949

Baxter, C and Crumley, J, *St Kilda – A Portrait of Britain's remotest island landscape*, Colin Baxter, 1988

Brown, G M, *Letters from Hamnavoe*, Savage, 2002

Buxton, B, *Mingulay: An Island and Its People*, Birlinn, 1995

Calhoun, M, *Exploring the Isles of the West*, Islands Book Trust, 2012

Campbell, J, *Millport and the Cumbraes*, North Ayrshire Council, 2004

Campbell, T, *Arran: A History*, Birlinn, 2007

Clarke, D and Maguire, P, *Skara Brae*, Historic Scotland, 2000

Fergusson, M, *George Mackay Brown: The Life*, John Murray, 2006

Finlayson, B, *Wild Harvesters: The First People in Scotland*, Birlinn, 1998

Fleet, C, *et al*, *Scotland – Mapping the Nation*, Birlinn, 2011

Harris, M P, *The Puffin*, T & AD Poyser, 1984

Haswell-Smith, H, *The Scottish Islands*, Canongate, 1996

Hedderwick, M, *Shetland Rambles – A Sketching Tour*, Birlinn, 2011
    An Eye on the Hebrides, Canongate, 1990

Holland, J, *Exploring the Islands of Scotland*, Frances Lincoln, 2011

Hume, R, RSPB *Complete Birds of Britain and Europe*, DK, 2002

Jarrold, *St Magnus Cathedral*, Jarrold Guide Books, 2007

Johnson, A, *Islands in the Sound: Wildlife in the Hebrides*, Gollancz, 1989

Latter, G, *Scottish Rock. Vol.2*, Pesda Press, 2009

Mackenzie, C, *Whisky Galore*, Birlinn, 2012

Mitchell, I, *Isles of the West*, Canongate, 1999
    Isles of the North, Birlinn, 2004

Mithen, S, *To the Islands*, TRP, 2010.

Morrison-Low, A D, *Northern Lights – The Age of Scottish Lighthouses*, National Museums Scotland, 2010

Murray, D S, *The Guga Hunters*, Birlinn, 2008

Newton, N, *The Isle of Bute*, Pevensey Island Guides, 1999

Nicolson, A, *Sea Room: An Island Life*, Harper Collins, 2001

Noble, G, *et al* (eds), *Scottish Odysseys – The Archaeology of Islands*, Tempus, 2008

Palsson, H and Edwards, P, (translated by) *Orkneyinga Saga: The History of the Earls of Orkney*, Penguin Classics, 1981

Rheinallt, T, Craik, C, Daw, P, Furness, B, Petty, S and Wood, D (eds), *Birds of Argyll*, Argyll Bird Club, 2007

Riddoch, L, *Riddoch on the Outer Hebrides*, Luath Press, 2007

Schalansky, J, *Atlas of Remote Islands*, Particular Books, 2010

Thomson, W, *The New History of Orkney*, Birlinn, 2008

Urquhart, J and Ellington, E, *Eigg*, Canongate, 1987

Wickham-Jones, C R, *Scotland's First Settlers*, Batsford, 1994
    Fear of Farming, Oxbow, 2010

Williams, R, *The Lords of the Isles*, House of Lochar, 1984

Wilson, B, *Stromness: a history*, The Orcadian, Kirkwall Press, 2013

Luath Press Limited

committed to publishing well written books worth reading

LUATH PRESS takes its name from Robert Burns, whose little collie Luath (*Gael.*, swift or nimble) tripped up Jean Armour at a wedding and gave him the chance to speak to the woman who was to be his wife and the abiding love of his life. Burns called one of 'The Twa Dogs' Luath after Cuchullin's hunting dog in Ossian's *Fingal*. Luath Press was established in 1981 in the heart of Burns country, and is now based a few steps up the road from Burns' first lodgings on Edinburgh's Royal Mile.

Luath offers you distinctive writing with a hint of unexpected pleasures.

Most bookshops in the UK, the US, Canada, Australia, New Zealand and parts of Europe either carry our books in stock or can order them for you. To order direct from us, please send a £sterling cheque, postal order, international money order or your credit card details (number, address of cardholder and expiry date) to us at the address below. Please add post and packing as follows: UK – £1.00 per delivery address; overseas surface mail – £2.50 per delivery address; overseas airmail – £3.50 for the first book to each delivery address, plus £1.00 for each additional book by airmail to the same address. If your order is a gift, we will happily enclose your card or message at no extra charge.

Luath Press Limited
543/2 Castlehill
The Royal Mile
Edinburgh EH1 2ND
Scotland

Telephone: 0131 225 4326 (24 hours)
Fax: 0131 225 4324
email: sales@luath.co.uk
Website: www.luath.co.uk